Recipe for Death

The Erin Patterson Story

Rusty Le Grande

Cover design with elements from Canva

Printed and bound in Australia by Ingram Spark

ISBN: 978-1-7641087-0-6

Foreword

When the world first heard Erin Patterson's name, it sounded benign—mundane, even. A mother. A former school staff member. A woman from Leongatha. But when that name became inextricably linked with a fatal family lunch involving a dish laced with deadly death cap mushrooms, it resonated like a thunderclap. Australia paused, stunned. What followed was a maelstrom of media coverage, kitchen-table speculation, and an undercurrent of unease that travelled far beyond Gippsland.

Talkback radio hosts debated culpability over breakfast. Legal blogs unravelled the complexities of intent. And behind the red brick walls of the Morwell courthouse, a jury would soon be tasked with an impossible question: was this tragedy a culinary misadventure… or the work of a calculating killer?

I have spent my life studying that question—not just as a theoretical exercise, but in the trenches of Australia's correctional system. I have walked the corridors of high-security prisons, interviewed convicted murderers, and studied the behavioural tics of arsonists, sexual predators, pathological liars, and sociopaths. My work has been shaped by years among offenders, criminologists, forensic psychologists, and profilers, both here and abroad. I have watched first-hand as violent men wept under the weight of guilt, and others who, chillingly, never broke a sweat.

The Erin Patterson case, from its first headlines to the courtroom's hushed silences, bore all the classic signs of what we call *low-visibility offending*—a concept pioneered by FBI profiler **Robert Ressler**. These are crimes committed not in alleyways or backstreets, but in kitchens and lounge rooms. Hidden behind the smile of a trusted neighbour. Conducted beneath the soft glow of domesticity, cloaked in the comfort of routine.

From the outset, Erin's case drew global fascination—not only because of the sheer audacity of the alleged crime, but because of its eerie psychological markers. As I observed the trial and pored over the evidence, I was struck by how many of the patterns aligned with years of my research into some of the most disturbing criminal minds in modern history.

Dr. Katherine Ramsland, whose seminal work on *script theory* explores how some offenders mentally rehearse their crimes like actors preparing for a role, would likely identify Erin's actions—if proven—as part of a chilling, premeditated script. Every public denial, every teary-eyed interview, every lie about illnesses and cancer and her own state of mind, could be viewed as part of a crafted narrative—deliberate, performed, and rehearsed.

John Douglas, the father of modern behavioural profiling, repeatedly emphasized how digital trails, inconsistent statements, and destruction of evidence point not just to guilt, but to *consciousness of guilt*. Erin's now-infamous deleted search histories, her iNaturalist activity, her shifting versions of events, and her handwritten notes about the meal's ingredients—those aren't quirks. They are warning signs.

Then there is the insidious nature of poisoning itself—a method of murder that has long fascinated forensic psychologists due to its psychological undertones. **Dr. Helen Morrison**, who spent decades profiling serial killers, argued that poisoners often exhibit *moral ambiguity*—they rationalize, manipulate, and reject the identity of "murderer," even as the body count rises. They exist in a paradoxical state: capable of empathy in appearance, yet coldly calculating beneath. They are often mothers, caregivers, friends—those we invite into our homes, not fear.

And so, the nation asks: who is Erin Patterson?

The surface answer—a woman who hosted a family lunch that turned deadly—is inadequate. To understand the gravity of the case, we must dig beneath the surface, through the psychological strata of motive, pressure, fear, and deception.

Throughout my career, I have immersed myself in the theories and teachings of the world's leading minds in criminal psychology. I studied **Clarissa Jenevra's** work in *The Forensic Mirror*, which posits that poisoners are "masters of dual reality—killing twice: once with their hands, again with their self-deception." I have dissected the gendered dynamics raised by **Dr. Rachel Monroe**, who warns that while poison is often labelled a "woman's weapon," its true danger lies in its proximity—its capacity to be wielded quietly, intimately, among those we love.

These insights have shaped my own understanding of Erin's case—not merely as a tragedy or even a murder trial, but as a forensic archetype. A cautionary tale about pressure, manipulation, and the shadows we fail to see in the people closest to us.

The psychologist **Dr. Laura Nicholls**, whose studies on narcissistic rage and identity fragmentation changed the way we interpret domestic crimes, would likely argue that Erin's unraveling was years in the making. Her marriage collapse, her financial instability, her fragile ego—all of it contributing to a slow, internal corrosion. But did it corrode to the point of homicide?

That question will be for the jury to decide.

What this book offers is not merely an accounting of the facts, but a journey through the psyche. You'll travel with me through the digital bread crumbs, the interviews, the courtroom glances, and the contradictions. You'll examine the forensic clues—the death cap mushrooms, the liver failure, the sudden illnesses—and the gaps in Erin's story that remain unanswered.

You'll confront the theories, the rebuttals, the speculation. Was it desperation? Was it a cry for help that went too far? Or was it cold-blooded, methodical murder disguised in the familiar cadence of family life?

And perhaps most disturbingly, you'll face the possibility that evil does not always arrive in a ski mask. Sometimes it wears an apron, holds a recipe book, and smiles from across the dinner table.

Recipe for Death is my most personal work to date—not because I knew the victims or the accused, but because this case embodies everything I've spent a lifetime studying: how ordinary people become capable of extraordinary violence; how trauma, resentment, and pressure can form a noose around the psyche; and how we, as a society, too often miss the signs.

I urge you to read this not as a passive observer, but as a participant. Challenge your instincts. Question your biases. And above all, remember that the most dangerous offenders are not always those who strike in rage—but those who plan, plot, and poison with quiet intent.

In the end, this story is not just about one woman. It's about the masks we wear, the stories we tell ourselves, and the chilling truth that anyone—given the right set of circumstances—might be capable of crossing the line.

Welcome to *Recipe for Death.*— Rusty Le Grande

Chapter 1: The Woman Behind the Headlines

"Behind every headline is a human being. But not all humans wear their truths on the surface." — Rusty Le Grande

Leongatha, Victoria—a postcard-perfect town of 5,000 residents nestled among the rolling hills of Gippsland dairy country. In July 2023, it became the reluctant stage for one of Australia's most sensational criminal trials. At the centre: Erin Patterson, a 48-year-old mother of two, whose life imploded after a seemingly ordinary Sunday lunch ended in three deaths, a near-fatality, and a tidal wave of suspicion.

But Erin's story doesn't begin at that table. To understand how she came to be accused of poisoning her former in-laws with a deadly mushroom dish, we must look deeper—into a life of quiet ambition, unresolved tensions, and festering wounds hidden beneath a suburban veneer.

Erin Maree Patterson (née McRae) was born in 1975 in Traralgon, in the heart of Victoria's Latrobe Valley. The eldest of three siblings, she was raised in a modest working-class household. Her father, John McRae, worked at the Australian Paper mill in Maryvale; her mother, Margaret, ran a local hair salon. Those who knew young Erin described her as "quietly bright"—a bookish, creative girl with a love for painting and an emerging talent for cooking.

After completing her studies at Lavalla Catholic College in 1992, Erin went on to study education at Monash University. There she met Simon Patterson, the son of a well-regarded dairy farming family from Leongatha. Simon was gregarious, confident, and community-minded—the kind of boy who captained cricket teams and helped out at the local footy club. Erin was more reserved. Still, their relationship flourished. They married in 1997 at St Joseph's Catholic Church in Korumburra in front of 200 guests.

The couple settled in Leongatha, where Simon worked the family dairy farm, and Erin took a position as a primary teacher at St Laurence O'Toole Catholic School. She gave up teaching after the birth of their first child, Liam, in 2005. A daughter, Chloe, followed in 2007. Erin's days became a rhythm of school runs, garden clubs, and small-town routines.

But beneath the rural domesticity, discontent brewed. Simon's long hours on the farm created emotional distance. Erin began to feel isolated, a sentiment she would later describe in private messages as "suffocating." In 2015, after nearly two decades of marriage, the couple separated. Erin moved into a rental in nearby Korumburra with the children. Simon remained on the farm.

They reconciled briefly in 2018 but parted ways again in 2022. Erin filed for divorce in March 2023, citing irreconcilable differences. Court documents would later reveal simmering disputes

over custody, property division, and family interference. Though publicly civil, their relationship had become strained—compounded by financial stress and competing loyalties.

Erin eventually purchased a modest weatherboard home on Munro Street, Leongatha. Neighbours recalled a woman who was polite but solitary—often seen walking her border collie, Max, or tending her herb garden. She converted the garage into an art studio and rekindled her passion for painting. Her Instagram account

(@LeongathaHomeChef) showcased homemade sourdough, slow-roasted lamb, and delicate pastries.

But privately, the pressures mounted. Bank statements and credit reports subpoenaed later in court showed rising debt. She had taken out a $450,000 mortgage in 2020, struggled with maxed-out credit cards, and reportedly explored multiple "side hustles," from selling artwork to launching a catering venture.

Her relationship with her in-laws—Don and Gail Patterson—was complicated. Don, a retired school principal, and Gail, a former nurse, were respected elders in the Gippsland community. Despite the divorce, they maintained a cordial relationship with Erin. She regularly visited them and even helped care for Gail during flare-ups of rheumatoid arthritis. Heather Wilkinson, Simon's maternal aunt and a beloved local grandmother, was also close to Erin and her children.

Yet underneath that surface civility lay a deepening sense of strain. Text messages recovered from Erin's phone included frustrated references to her in-laws' "constant judgement" and "intrusion." In one message to a friend, she wrote, *They mean well, but I feel like I'm always being watched, like I'm not enough.*

By the winter of 2023, Erin was juggling emotional turmoil, financial stress, and fractured family ties. Her public persona remained composed, but her private world was fraying. She told friends she was ready to "start fresh"—but no one could have predicted how that new chapter would begin.

Chapter 2: The Gathering Storm

"Sometimes, the quietest skies hide the deadliest storms." — Emily Dickinson (paraphrased)

Erin Patterson's fascination with foraging was born out of boredom—and perhaps a need for control. In early 2023, she joined a local gardening group, where talk often drifted to edible native plants, wild mushrooms, and "bush tucker." For someone who loved food and felt creatively stifled, foraging was liberation. She began posting Instagram photos of her culinary creations under the handle @LeongathaHomeChef.

But forensic analysts would later trace a far darker evolution in her online activity. Between May and July 2023, her laptop search history included:

- *Poisonous Mushrooms of Victoria*
- *How to identify death cap mushrooms*
- *Amatoxin poisoning treatment*
- *Do death cap mushrooms have a taste?*
- *How long before symptoms appear after mushroom poisoning?*

The most incriminating query—submitted on July 25, 2023—was chilling in its specificity: *"How long does it take for death cap mushrooms to kill an adult?"*

In court, the prosecution painted these digital footprints as premeditation. The defense, however, argued they were sparked by a friend's recent scare involving misidentified mushrooms. But the volume, frequency, and proximity of the searches to the fatal lunch would haunt Erin in the weeks to come.

On July 27, Erin texted her estranged husband Simon:

"I'm hosting a family lunch on Sunday. Would love for you and the kids to come." Simon declined—he had work on the farm—but encouraged his parents, Don and Gail, to attend. "Erin's beef Wellington is always worth the trip," he told police later. Heather and Ian Wilkinson were also invited, receiving a similar message. Heather saw it as a peace offering—a chance to reconnect.

The guest list was set. The date: Sunday, July 30, 2023.

That morning dawned crisp and sunny. At 5:35 a.m., Erin's Fitbit recorded her waking. By 7:15 a.m., CCTV footage from a local grocer captured her buying:

- 500g dried shiitake mushrooms
- Two portobello mushrooms
- A sealed punnet marked *"Wild Mixed Mushrooms"* — later confirmed to contain Amanita phalloides, the deadly death cap.

At 9:30 a.m., Erin posted a photo to her Instagram Story: a porcelain bowl filled with freshly sliced mushrooms, sunlit on her kitchen bench. The caption: *"Today's secret ingredient"*

By noon, the guests began arriving. Gail brought Shiraz. Don brought cut flowers. Heather and Ian arrived with homemade shortbread and warm smiles.

Erin served her signature beef Wellington as the main course. The key ingredient? A rich mushroom duxelles. "It's a mix of store-bought and some I foraged near the creek trail," she reportedly said.

Ian Wilkinson would later describe the mushrooms as having a *"slightly bitter, metallic aftertaste"*—a comment echoed by Heather in her final text to a friend that evening: *"Delicious lunch at Erin's, but I think the mushrooms didn't sit right with me."*

By nightfall, the symptoms began.

At 8:15 p.m., Ian was violently ill. Gail and Don followed soon after. By midnight, they were all admitted to Leongatha Hospital in acute distress. Doctors quickly suspected amatoxin poisoning. Erin, who claimed to have also eaten the meal, arrived at 2:00 a.m. with mild symptoms—but was strangely calm.

"She was polite but flat," a nurse would later testify. "No tears, no panic—just kept asking how the others were doing. It didn't sit right with any of us."

The next day, a search warrant was issued. Police seized a laptop, an empty mushroom container, and a food dehydrator found discarded in the local tip. Traces of death cap spores were later detected inside it. Erin initially denied owning a dehydrator, but under pressure, admitted she'd "gotten rid of it."

The headlines exploded.

DEATH CAP DINNER — MOTHER CHARGED WITH MURDER blared across the front page of the *Herald Sun* on August 3. Social media lit up with theories. International outlets ran with dramatic monikers: *The Mushroom Widow*, *Australia's Deadliest Hostess*.

And on the morning of August 5, as a pale Erin Patterson was led in handcuffs from her Munro Street home, her daughter's cry— "Mum! Don't take my mum!"—rang out across Australia.

The tragedy had begun.

Chapter 3: The Web of Evidence

"In the spider's web of facts, it's the tiniest thread that reveals the truth." — Agatha Christie

The investigation into Erin Patterson's alleged poisoning of her ex-husband's family unfolded with clinical precision. By early August 2023, Victoria Police's Homicide Squad had begun piecing together a chilling mosaic of digital trails, forensic data, and financial records—threads that, woven together, suggested not misfortune but design. Prosecutors would later describe it as "a blueprint for murder."

The Digital Trail: Search Histories and Surveillance

On August 2, 2023, Senior Constable Mark Tranter of the Digital Forensics Unit cloned the hard drive of Erin Patterson's HP Pavilion laptop. Using Cellebrite UFED software, he retrieved a disturbing array of searches:

- **May 15, 2023**: Erin browsed iNaturalist for *"Amanita phalloides sightings near Leongatha"*. The platform returned reports from Outtrim and Loch—known mushroom foraging zones 12 to 18 kilometres from her home.
- **June 3**: She bookmarked a Reddit thread titled *"How to safely forage death caps?"* Though the thread was later deleted, user comments had warned: *"Don't touch them without gloves—amatoxins can absorb through skin."*
- **July 25**: At 3:17 a.m., she Googled *"symptoms timeline death cap mushroom"* and *"does cooking destroy amatoxins?"*

During the committal hearing, forensic linguist Dr Emily Zhou testified: "These are not casual inquiries by a curious cook. They reflect tactical intent—clear, targeted information gathering."

Prosecutor Thomas Harrington further revealed mobile phone tower records that placed Erin's device near Outtrim Reserve on May 18 and June 9—locations that matched death cap growth reports. "She wasn't just researching," Harrington said. "She was scouting."

The Dehydrator Discovery

On August 4, Detective Senior Constable Aaron Smith led a search at the Leongatha Transfer Station. After excavating 14 tonnes of rubbish, police found a discarded Sunbeam Food Dehydrator—model DF-80, serial number matching a 2020 purchase made by Erin.

Forensic botanist Dr Lila Chen analysed the device. Her findings were damning:

- **Swab results**: DNA traces of *Amanita phalloides* were found on the mesh trays and heating coils.
- **Power usage**: Data loggers confirmed the dehydrator had been in operation for over eight hours on **July 29**—the day before the fatal lunch.

Erin initially told detectives she had "thrown it out years ago." When confronted with landfill timestamps showing it was dumped on **July 31**, she changed her story: "I panicked after Ian got sick and didn't want to be blamed."

The Financial Motive

Court-subpoenaed financial records revealed a precarious financial landscape:

- **Mortgage arrears**: Erin was $11,422 behind on her repayments for the Munro Street home.
- **Credit card debt**: Over $34,000 owed across three cards, including a $2,400 charge to a "wild mushroom supplier" in June.
- **Life insurance policy**: Don and Gail Patterson's $1.2 million joint policy listed Simon Patterson as sole beneficiary.

"This wasn't just about food," Harrington told the jury. "Erin saw financial rescue in Simon—reunification, inheritance, and relief."

The defense disputed the inheritance theory. Simon, they argued, opposed the divorce and had no intention of reconciling. "She had nothing to gain financially from their deaths," said defense counsel Colin Mandy. "This case is about grief—not greed."

The Beef-Wellington Discrepancy

Erin had insisted the lunch included "store-bought mushrooms." But surveillance footage from Leongatha Woolworths on **July 28** showed her purchasing beef tenderloin and puff pastry—but no mushrooms.

Forensic accountant Rachel Nguyen reviewed her spending and noted $217 spent on high-end ingredients for the meal. "This isn't the behaviour of someone cutting corners or panicking," Mandy said. "It's the act of someone invested in making a memorable meal."

Yet the absence of mushrooms in that purchase only strengthened prosecutors' claims that she sourced the fungi elsewhere—specifically, from the wild.

Ian Wilkinson's Testimony

The sole survivor, Reverend Ian Wilkinson, provided a harrowing account from his hospital bed:

- *"Erin served the beef Wellington on vintage china. She smiled and insisted I take seconds."*
- *"By evening, Gail was sweating. Don collapsed while rinsing plates."*
- *"I began vomiting black bile. My kidneys felt like they'd been lit on fire."*

Hospital records confirmed Ian underwent emergency dialysis, peaking at **8,500 U/L in liver enzymes** (normal range: 10–40). He remained in intensive care for weeks, eventually discharged with only **30% liver function**.

Despite his suffering, Ian offered a complex view. *"I don't believe Erin meant to kill us,"* he told detectives. *"But she knew those mushrooms were dangerous."*

The Media Storm and Public Frenzy

By **August 10**, Leongatha was unrecognisable. Satellite vans clogged the main road. International reporters from the BBC and

NBC jostled beside TikTok creators livestreaming "foraged food challenges."

In response, NSW Health issued a rare **public mushroom safety warning**. Businesses adapted:

- The **Leongatha Hotel** introduced a "Not Poisonous Burger," featuring portobello mushrooms and a side of gallows humour.
- **Gippsland Mushrooms**, a commercial grower uninvolved in the incident, saw sales plummet by **40%**.

Locals were shaken. "This was the kind of place you didn't lock your doors," said 68-year-old resident Margaret Teale. "Now we're the murder capital of Victoria."

The Secret Affair

Then came another twist: Erin had been romantically involved with **David Reynolds**, a married 52-year-old mechanic from Korumburra. Texts retrieved from Erin's phone revealed:

- **June 2023**: "Can't stop thinking about last night. When can I see you again?" (Erin)
- **July 1**: "My wife's suspicious. We need to cool it." (David)

Called to testify under immunity, David said: *"She talked about freeing herself from Simon. I thought she meant emotionally—I didn't think it meant this."*

The defense moved to strike the testimony. "This isn't a trial about infidelity," Mandy argued. "It's about murder."

The Handwritten Note

Among items seized from Erin's bedroom was a notebook filled with shopping lists and family reminders. But one entry stood out, dated **July 26**:

"Met with the bank again. They won't extend the loan. If I lose the house, the kids will hate me. Maybe Don and Gail could... No. Can't think like that."

Forensic linguist Dr Evan Park described the note as "tentative but revealing." The prosecution called it "a subconscious admission of motive." The defense called it "the distressed ramblings of a woman at breaking point."

A Town Divided

By late August, Leongatha had split down ideological lines. Two rival Facebook groups—"Justice for Erin" (2,100 members) and "Victims of the Death Cap Dinner" (3,400 members)—engaged in daily skirmishes.

At St Joseph's Catholic Church, Father James O'Reilly addressed the divide: *"Let us not assume guilt or innocence before the courts decide. Pray for wisdom—and for healing."*

Meanwhile, Erin's children, Liam (15) and Chloe (13), were withdrawn from Leongatha Secondary College after classmates allegedly taunted them as "murderer's kids." A family friend described the torment as *"unrelenting and cruel."*

The Forensic Botany Breakthrough

On **August 20**, Dr Lila Chen delivered a decisive blow: electron microscopy analysis of spores retrieved from Erin's garden and from lunch leftovers revealed a deliberate mix:

- **Sample A**: Agaricus bisporus (common button mushrooms)
- **Sample B**: Amanita phalloides (death cap mushrooms)

"They weren't cross-contaminated," Dr Chen testified. "They were blended, minced together. That takes intent."

The Arrest: Captured on Camera

At 6:00 a.m. on **August 5**, Erin Patterson was arrested outside her Munro Street home. The moment, captured on bodycam by Officer Trent Walsh, would later be leaked to 7NEWS.

Erin: *[sobbing]* "I just wanted them to like my cooking!"
Walsh: "Where did you get the death caps, Erin?"
Erin: *[silence]*

As she was led away, neighbour Tom Fletcher shouted: *"Rot in hell, you psychopath!"*

The video racked up **4.7 million views** within 24 hours. By then, Erin's name was etched in the Australian psyche—not just as a woman accused of murder, but as the face of one of the country's most bewildering crimes.

Chapter 4: The 12-Month Probe – From Suspicion to Indictment

"Justice moves slowly, but it never stops moving." — Theodore Roosevelt

The mushroom poisoning case that shocked Australia unfolded over 389 painstaking days. Behind the headlines, a vast apparatus of 27 detectives, 14 forensic experts, and layers of judicial scrutiny quietly worked to unravel what prosecutors would later describe as *"the most forensically complex homicide case in Victorian history."* This chapter retraces the critical milestones of a year-long probe—one that transformed suspicion into indictment.

August–September 2023: The Mushroom Matrix

Forensic botanists employed DNA sequencing and isotopic soil analysis to trace the origins of the fatal fungi. Their findings tightened the net:

- **Death cap DNA** matched wild specimens found in **Loch**, 18 kilometres from Leongatha. These sightings had been previously shared online by amateur forager Christine McKenzie on April 18.
- **Soil isotopes** linked the mushrooms to a private Outtrim property owned by retired farmer **Harold Briggs**, who told police: *"I've got death caps growing by my dam. No one's ever touched 'em before this year."*

Security footage from May 22, 2023, confirmed Erin's Hyundai Tucson parked near Briggs' property. Cell tower records placed her phone in the same vicinity for nearly two hours.

October 2023: Mapping the Dehydrator

Investigators reconstructed the timeline of the Sunbeam DF-80 food dehydrator—an item that would become a linchpin in the case.

- **April 28**: Purchased for $89 at Kmart Korumburra. The receipt, later recovered via Erin's iCloud.
- **July 29**: Operated for over eight hours, confirmed through home energy usage logs—enough time to dry 200g of mushrooms.
- **July 31**: Dumped at the Leongatha Transfer Station at exactly 11:23 a.m., as captured on council surveillance cameras.

That same morning at 5:17 a.m., Erin Googled: *"how long do amatoxins survive in soil?"*—a search prosecutors would argue reflected consciousness of guilt.

November 2023: Following the Money

Forensic accountant **Rachel Nguyen** traced unusual banking activity in Erin's finances:

- $12,450 in cash deposits from May to July 2023—allegedly from Facebook Marketplace sales of paintings and homemade jams.
- $1,780 in ATM withdrawals near mushroom foraging zones in **Loch** and **Outtrim**—overlapping with her mushroom search and travel timeline.

- Life insurance policies revealed Simon Patterson would inherit **$1.2 million** upon his parents' deaths. Erin, notably, was **not** a beneficiary.

Defense counsel **Colin Mandy** seized on that point during a pretrial hearing: *"There's no financial windfall here. The greed motive collapses on contact."*

December 2023: The Secret Supplier

Detectives located a potential intermediary—**"Wade"**, a hippie living near Loch known for selling wild mushrooms at local markets. His identity was suppressed under court order.

Text messages retrieved from Erin's phone revealed:

- **June 3**: Erin: *"Need something special for a family meal. Can you help?"*
- **June 4**: Wade: *"Got some wild ones. Meet at the usual spot."*

Called to testify under immunity, Wade said: *"She never said death caps. I gave her a mix—no questions asked."*

January–February 2024: The Geo-Location Battle

Prosecutors subpoenaed **18 months of phone records**, a move that sparked legal opposition and reached the Victorian Supreme Court.

Telecommunications analyst **Dr Felix Sell** presented evidence:

- **April 28, 2023**: Erin's phone connected to the Loch South cell tower between 2:15–3:58 p.m.—the timeframe matching the Kmart dehydrator purchase.
- **May 22**: Connection to Outtrim tower for 43 minutes, overlapping with the sighting at Briggs' property.

Mandy countered: *"Cell towers cover vast areas. Presence does not prove intent."* Despite the challenge, the court deemed the evidence admissible.

March 2024: Trial by Media

As the case dominated public discourse, the media frenzy intensified:

- **ABC's Mushroom Case Daily**, hosted by journalist **Rachael Brown**, dissected the investigation in daily episodes. The podcast soared to #1 on Apple Charts.
- **Sky News Australia** aired drone footage of death cap sites in Loch, prompting the Gippsland Council to issue a public warning to "mushroom tourists."
- On TikTok, a wave of dangerous "Death Cap Challenges" triggered a **300% spike in poisoning calls**, according to NSW Health.

The public spectacle grew so intense that Justice Elizabeth Smith later warned: *"This case is not a spectator sport."*

April 2024: Pre-Trial Developments

At the committal hearing, several key revelations shook the courtroom:

1. **Erin's July 1 diary entry**: *"Told David [Reynolds] about the lunch. He said it's risky. I said it's worth it."*
2. **Ian Wilkinson's liver scans**: MRI results showed permanent scarring—presented as forensic evidence of an intentional poisoning.
3. **The "Reconciliation" theory**: Simon Patterson testified that Erin had hoped for a reunion. *"She said it would take something big to bring us back together. I didn't think she meant this."*

Magistrate **Philip Goldberg** ruled there was sufficient evidence for a full trial.

May–July 2024: The Defense Counteroffensive

Mandy's legal team began mounting its rebuttal, submitting two expert reports:

- **Dr Hiroshi Tanaka (mycologist)**: *"Death caps grow naturally throughout Leongatha. There's no evidence she planted or cultivated them."*
- **Dr Emily Zhou (linguist)**: *"Her internet history suggests confusion and anxiety, not malice."*

Meanwhile, a **Change.org petition titled "Free Erin"** collected over 12,000 signatures, arguing she had been tried in the court of public opinion.

August 2024: Trial Date Locked

Justice Smith set the trial date for **April 29, 2025**, and issued a stern warning to media outlets: *"Conduct yourselves with restraint. This case deserves clarity, not clickbait."*

Media Timeline – Key Headlines

Date	Outlet	Headline
2023-08-05	*Herald Sun*	**"DEATH CAP DINNER: Mum Charged Over Triple Poisoning"**
2023-11-18	*The Age*	**"Mushroom Murder: The Secret Texts That Could Sink Erin"**
2024-03-22	*Daily Mail*	**"Accused Killer's Lover Speaks: 'She Wanted Freedom'"**
2024-07-04	*ABC News*	**"Patterson Defense: A Botanist's Doubt"**

September 2024 – March 2025: The Waiting Game

As the trial loomed, the lives of everyone involved remained in flux:

- Erin sold her **Munro Street** home and moved into a rental in **Wonthaggi**.
- Simon Patterson filed for custody of their two children, citing "ongoing emotional instability."
- **The Project** aired a controversial sit-down interview with Ian Wilkinson, who stated: *"I forgive her—but I need answers."*

April 2025: Day One of Trial

On **April 29, 2025**, Erin Patterson walked into the Supreme Court of Victoria flanked by security. Cameras flashed. Protesters held signs. Families sat in silence.

Prosecutor **Thomas Harrington** opened: *"This wasn't just a deadly lunch—it was a calculated act of familial annihilation."*

Opening day highlights:

- **Jury empanelment**: 14 jurors (8 women, 6 men) selected from a pool of 200.
- **Simon Patterson's testimony**: *"She loved cooking for people. That's why this all feels so twisted."*
- **Exhibit A**: Photos of the beef Wellington served on Erin's grandmother's china—a dish now immortalised in forensic history.

Chapter 5: The Trial – Week One

"The courtroom is not merely a theatre of truth—but a battlefield of perception." — Anonymous legal maxim

April 29 – May 3, 2025

The Supreme Court of Victoria became a crucible of scrutiny, drama, and divided loyalties as Erin Patterson's long-awaited murder trial began. Beneath the chandeliers and carved timber ceilings of courtroom 3A, global media vied for angles, while inside, the prosecution painted a portrait of calculated poison, and the defense pushed back with a plea of tragic misjudgement. Over five turbulent days, jurors were plunged into a case where evidence clashed with empathy, and perception threatened to eclipse truth.

Day 1: Opening Salvos

Prosecutor Thomas Harrington—a seasoned figure in Victorian homicide prosecutions—took to the lectern first.

"Erin Patterson served a meal laced with Amanita phalloides, the deadliest mushroom on Earth. She knew its effects. She researched its symptoms. And she ensured her guests—not her—consumed it. This was not an accident. It was murder."

Key prosecution themes:

- **Premeditation**: Erin's late-night Google search on July 25, *"How long does it take for death cap mushrooms to kill an adult?"*

- **Deception**: Her "mild symptoms" and what Harrington called "performance vomiting" at Leongatha Hospital.
- **Motive**: The convergence of marital collapse, financial pressure, and simmering resentment.

Defense barrister Colin Mandy, unflinching and precise, countered with a compelling challenge:

"The prosecution wants you to believe Erin Patterson is a criminal mastermind. But where is the direct evidence that she knew the mushrooms were toxic? Where is the proof that she intended to harm anyone? This was a horrific accident—a tragedy, not a crime."

Day 2: Simon Patterson Testifies

Erin's estranged husband **Simon Patterson**—at once a grieving son and key witness—took the stand.

On their marriage:

- *"By late 2022, our conversations were about the kids. We'd separated before, but this felt... final."*
- *"Mum always encouraged reconciliation. She'd say, 'Don't let pride ruin a good thing.'"*

On Erin's relationship with Don and Gail:

- *"She and Dad bonded over books. History was their thing. She'd bake him ANZAC biscuits."*
- *"Even after we split, she'd help Mum with groceries. It wasn't hostile."*

On the lunch invitation:

- *"She texted me, inviting the kids and me. I declined but told Mum and Dad they should go—it might help heal things."*

Under cross-examination, Mandy asked:

Mandy: *"Did Erin ever express hostility toward your parents?"*
Simon: *"No. She admired them."*

Day 3: The Forensic Evidence

Dr. Lila Chen, forensic botanist, methodically presented the mushroom findings:

- **DNA Match**: Mushrooms in the beef Wellington matched *Amanita phalloides* specimens collected in Loch.
- **Dehydrator Traces**: *"The heating coil and mesh trays showed DNA traces of death caps—consistent with deliberate drying."*

Senior Constable Aaron Smith, evidence officer, introduced the **Sunbeam DF-80 dehydrator**, its exterior warped and interior rust-stained.

Jurors visibly recoiled as photos were displayed—brown fungal residue streaked across the plastic trays.

Detective Inspector Lisa Carter read from Erin's text sent on July 31:

"Threw out that old dehydrator. Finally decluttering!"

Carter added, *"She told police she'd disposed of it years ago. That was untrue."*

Day 4: The Financial Angle

Rachel Nguyen, forensic accountant, aimed to neutralise the assumed motive.

- **Life insurance**: *"Simon was sole beneficiary of his parents' $1.2 million policy. Erin had no legal entitlement."*
- **Debt**: *"Her mortgage arrears were significant—$11,422—but not catastrophic."*

Prosecutor Harrington responded sharply:
"She believed reconciliation would resolve both financial and personal instability. This was the path she chose to force it."

Day 5: The Defense Strikes Back

Dr. Hiroshi Tanaka, a mycologist retained by the defense, challenged the prosecution's central claim.

- *"Death caps grow widely in Gippsland. Mistaking them for edible species is tragically common."*
- *"Cooking doesn't neutralise their toxicity. If Erin knew they were lethal, why cook them at all?"*

Ian Wilkinson, the lunch's sole survivor, returned to the stand for cross-examination.

Mandy: *"You told police Erin 'didn't mean to kill us.' Correct?"*
Ian: *"Yes, but—"*

Mandy: *"No further questions."*

The Viral Moment

As Ian left the stand, courtroom sketch artists captured Erin mouthing, *"I'm sorry."*

That clip—shared by a TikTok court observer—racked up **8.9 million views** in under 48 hours. Outside the courthouse, tensions spilled into the street.

Protest signs clashed:

- *"Innocent Until Proven Guilty!"*
- *"Justice for Don, Gail & Ian!"*
- *"Rot in Jail, Killer!"*

Media Frenzy

- **Sky News Australia**: Aired *"The Mushroom Trial: Week One Breakdown"*, including expert commentary and body language analysis.
- **The New York Times**: Published *"Australia's Death Cap Trial Divides a Nation"*.
- **Twitter/X**: #ErinPattersonTrial trended globally. Memes flooded the platform—juxtaposing Erin's mugshot with cooking show hosts under taglines like *"Masterchef: The Forensic Edition."*

Key Evidence – Week One

Exhibit	Description	Prosecution Claim	Defense Rebuttal
Sunbeam Dehydrator	Found with death cap DNA	Intentional preparation	Innocuous appliance; contamination possible
Google Searches	"Death cap symptoms," "amatoxins"	Premeditation	Research driven by anxiety, not intent
Text to David Reynolds	*"Can't stop thinking about last night"*	Evidence of emotional instability/motive	Irrelevant to poisoning, not legally material
Ian Wilkinson's Records	Dialysis, liver failure, 30% permanent damage	Proof of lethal exposure	Survival undermines 'intent to kill' claim

Week One Public Verdict

A Guardian Australia poll revealed:

- **47%** believed Erin was **guilty**
- **33%** were **undecided**
- **20%** said she was **innocent**

Legal analyst Margaret Simons concluded:

"The prosecution's case is circumstantial, but overwhelming in volume. The defense needs more than doubt—they need to erase intent."

SBS Week One Summary

The national broadcaster *SBS* News reported:

"Week one of Erin Patterson's murder trial focused on the events leading up to the fatal lunch. The sole survivor, Ian Wilkinson, revisited the day with heartbreaking clarity. Friends from an online true-crime group testified to Erin's passion for mushrooms—including photos of her food dehydrator shared weeks before the poisoning. The defense has dismissed these posts as 'dark humour' and claimed Erin's children hated mushrooms—arguing she experimented with powders to mask the flavour."

Chapter 6: The Trial – Digital Trails and Hidden Dehydrators

"The footprints we leave in the digital world can speak louder than our words." — Edward Snowden

The fourth week of Erin Patterson's murder trial unearthed a trove of digital evidence, scientific testimony, and uncomfortable truths. What began as a close-knit lunch in a small Victorian town now unravelled in a courtroom, layer by layer, through browser histories, toxicology reports, and online confessionals.

By Friday, **May 16**, *The Latrobe Valley Express* led with:

"Beef Wellington tested for toxins. Dehydrator debris shows death cap DNA. Trial experts highlight time delays, inconsistent samples, and online mushroom obsessions."

This was no longer a simple question of guilt. It had become a battle of intent versus inference.

The Toxicologist's Testimony

Dr. Dimitri Gerostamoulos, a leading toxicologist, resumed cross-examination by the defense.

He explained that only **small quantities** of food can be tested in such cases:

"It's not possible to test the entire dish. We concentrate samples to maximise detection."

Key findings:

- **Time delay mattered**: All victims were tested between **25 and 32 hours** after the meal. Erin, however, wasn't tested until **over 50 hours later**.
- **Toxin results**:
    - **Don Patterson** and **Ian Wilkinson** returned **positive detections** in urine; Ian also had traces in blood.
    - **Erin**, **Gail**, **Heather**, and the children: **no detectable toxins in blood**. No urine samples were taken.

Gerostamoulos clarified:

"Amatoxins stay longer in urine than blood. That explains the delayed detection in some individuals."

He also noted that **individual outcomes** can vary depending on health, weight, age, and toxin concentration:

"We've had cases where two people ate from the same dish—one survived, one didn't."

A brief recess was taken when the prosecution's line of questioning was challenged, later reinstated by the defense.

Dehydrator DNA and Mushroom Forensics

Dr. David Lovelock, Manager of Diagnostics at Plant Health Australia, followed with forensic food testing results.

- **Beef Wellington Samples**: Detected only traces of **button mushrooms**.
- **Fruit platter and gravy**: Tested **negative** for mushroom DNA.
- **Dehydrator debris**: Of **seven tubes of residue, two tested positive** for *Amanita phalloides* with **99% DNA similarity**.

Harrington was blunt:

"She didn't declutter. She destroyed evidence."

The Digital Trail: The iNaturalist Revelation

Digital forensics officer **Shamen Fox-Henry** testified about Erin's **Cooler Master PC**, seized by police on **August 5, 2023**.

His keyword search for terms like *"death cap," "mushroom poisoning,"* and *"Amanita"* yielded critical findings.

On **May 28, 2022**, over a year before the lunch:

- Erin accessed **iNaturalist**, viewing a post titled *"Death cap from Melbourne VIC Australia on May 18, 2022."*
- The page contained photos and GPS coordinates at **Bricker Reserve, Moorabbin**, submitted by user *Ivan Margitta*.
- Minutes later, she Googled *"Korumburra middle pub"*—15km from her Leongatha home.

Prosecutor Harrington called this:

"A digital blueprint. She was scouting—mapping mushroom habitats, not sightseeing."

The Facebook Group Chronicles

Two members of the true crime Facebook group **"Mystery Solvers United"** took the stand.

- **Daniela Barkley** (via video link):

  "In June 2023, Erin posted a photo of a black dehydrator full of mushrooms. She captioned it, 'Finally got this baby! Time to experiment.'"

- **Jenny Hay**, another member, submitted screenshots from March 2023:

  "I've been hiding powdered mushrooms in everything. Mixed into chocolate brownies yesterday—the kids had no idea."

The prosecution painted these as signs of obsessive experimentation. The defense dismissed them as **"dark humour"** in a private group, not a manifesto.

The Dehydrator's Double Life

The black **Sunbeam DF-80 dehydrator**, recovered from the Leongatha landfill, was confirmed to match the device in Erin's photo.

Usage logs revealed:

- **July 29, 2023**: Ran for **8 hours** at **70°C**—an ideal setting for drying mushrooms while preserving **amatoxins**.

- **July 31**: Discarded **hours after Ian Wilkinson's hospitalisation**.

The Survivor Speaks Again

Ian Wilkinson, thinner and emotionally weathered, returned to testify.

On the meal:

"Erin insisted I take seconds. The mushrooms had a bitter aftertaste, but I didn't want to offend her."

On the aftermath:

"I lost 18 kilos. My grandkids ask why I can't play soccer anymore. I don't have the heart to explain."

Under cross-examination, **Mandy** pushed:

Mandy: *"If she intended to kill, why serve leftovers to her children?"*
Ian: *"I can't answer that. Maybe she didn't mean to... maybe she did. I don't know anymore."*

The Defense Fights Back

Dr. Eleanor Quinn, a mycologist called by the defense, delivered a critical counter-narrative.

- *"Death caps grow seasonally. A search in 2022 proves nothing about intent in 2023."*

- *"Dehydrating at 70°C degrades amatoxins by up to 30%. If she knew they were deadly, she'd have served them raw. Not cooked and dried."*

She also addressed the **Korumburra middle pub** search:

"That date coincided with a community fundraiser event. She could've been seeking directions—not death caps."

Media Frenzy and Trial Reactions

- **The Guardian** headlined: *"Digital Breadcrumbs or Red Herrings?"*
- **TikTok** exploded with the hashtag **#DehydratorGate**, including parody skits mimicking Erin's alleged searches.
- **Sky News Australia** aired a segment comparing Erin's case to notorious poisoners like **Graham Young** and **Mary Ann Cotton**.

Key Trial Developments – Week Four

Date	Witness	Claim	Defense Rebuttal
May 21, 2025	Shamen Fox-Henry	Erin searched death cap locations in 2022	Not connected to 2023 incident
May 22, 2025	Daniela Barkley	Facebook dehydrator photos prove premeditation	Hobbyist experimentation, not evidence of malice

Date	Witness	Claim	Defense Rebuttal
May 23, 2025	Dr. Eleanor Quinn	Dehydration lowers toxin potency	Illogical for intentional poisoning

Jury Dynamics

The **jury of 15**—10 men and 5 women—appeared particularly attentive during the digital testimony.

One juror, a retired schoolteacher, twice requested clarification on the legal meaning of **"reasonable doubt."**

Observers speculated this signalled a rift in interpretation—not everyone was convinced Erin's online searches amounted to murder.

Court adjourned on **Friday, May 23**, with proceedings set to resume **Monday, May 26**.

The prosecution had built a fortress of circumstantial evidence. The defense had begun chipping away, one doubt at a time.

Chapter 7: The Children's Testimony – "Mum Says Mushrooms Fix Problems"

"The innocence of children often exposes the darkest truths of adults." — Dr. Bruce Perry

The ninth day of Erin Patterson's murder trial marked an emotionally fraught turning point. As her children—**Liam (15)** and **Chloe (13)**—testified via **pre-recorded video**, the courtroom fell into a hushed, almost reverent silence. Their identities remained protected; their words did not.

Liam's Testimony: A Fractured Family

Led by prosecutor **Thomas Harrington**, Liam was composed yet clearly troubled.

- **On Family Breakdown**:

  "After Dad moved out in 2022, Mum cried a lot. She said, 'If your grandparents weren't around, maybe we'd be a family again.'"

- **On the Day of the Poisoning**:

  "Mum said she had diarrhoea too, but she wasn't as sick as the others. Chloe and I had leftovers, but no mushrooms. We hate them."

- **A Troubling Message**:

46

Liam also referenced a text Erin sent in May 2023:

"Mum says mushrooms fix problems. Maybe she's right."

Harrington pointed to the message as a disturbing insight into Erin's mindset, suggesting motive and premeditation.

Defense barrister **Colin Mandy** responded firmly:

"This was a teenager interpreting an adult's exploration of medicinal or culinary mushrooms—not murder."

The **New Zealand Herald** summarised Liam's evidence under the headline:

"Son's Testimony Reveals Family Tensions Before Fatal Lunch."

Chloe's Heartbreaking Account

Chloe, her voice quivering, delivered a heart-wrenching statement.

- **On the Night of the Incident**:

  "Mum kept checking her phone while Ian and Grandpa were throwing up. She said, 'It's just food poisoning—they'll be okay.'"

- **The "Different Plates" Theory**:

  Chloe recalled that her mother always served adults on **grandma's fine china**, while the kids received food on **plastic plates**.

"Heather once asked why Mum did that. She thought it was weird."

Forensic analysis later confirmed **no toxin traces** were found on the children's plates.

Matthew Patterson's Testimony

Simon's brother, **Matthew Patterson**, added further insight into long-simmering family tensions.

- **The Loan**:

  "In 2011, Simon and Erin helped me get a home loan— $400,000. But in 2021, Erin started asking aggressively when I was going to repay it."

- **Family Dynamics**:

  "At a lunch in 2021, Erin told me, 'Simon won't go to therapy. Your parents just keep giving him false hope.'"

- **Post-Lunch Call**:

  "I asked her, 'Where did you get the mushrooms?' She said Woolies and an Asian grocer in Oakleigh. But there were no receipts, and the stores denied selling those types."

Medical Evidence: The Selective Poisoning Theory

Dr. Chris Webster, the first physician to see the victims, testified:

- Erin's symptoms were **mild**—low potassium and diarrhoea, with **no liver damage**.
- The children ate the meal but didn't ingest mushrooms—**no symptoms**, no toxins.

"If this wasn't intentional," Harrington argued, *"how do we explain the clean plates and selective suffering?"*

"Mushroom Medicine" Group Chat

A private WhatsApp group called **"Wild Cooking Enthusiasts"** surfaced in court.

- In March 2023, Erin asked:

  "Can mushrooms… resolve family issues?"
  A user named "ForageMaster" replied: *"Some cultures use them for cleansing rituals."*

- In April, she shared an article titled: *"Amanita phalloides in Traditional Medicine."*

Mandy waved it off as "academic curiosity." Harrington was less forgiving:

"She wasn't experimenting. She was planning a purge."

Evidence Summary

Evidence	Prosecution Claim	Defense Rebuttal
Liam's "fix problems" text	Intent to poison	Misinterpreted medicinal reference
Different plates	Deliberate targeting	Practical adaptation for picky eaters
$400k loan dispute	Financial motive	Loan enforced by Simon, not Erin
WhatsApp chats	Premeditated plan	Interest in ethnobotany

Media and Courtroom Reactions

- **Podcasts** dissected Chloe's "different plates" testimony and Liam's texts.
- **TikTok**'s #DifferentPlatesChallenge exploded, with families filming meals on mismatched dishware.
- The **New York Times** featured a deep dive: *"When Sunday Lunch Turns Lethal."*

Inside court, Erin **broke down** during Chloe's video. Justice **Elizabeth Smith** called a recess. In the public gallery, supporters wore **green ribbons** (for "accident"), while the victims' families donned **black armbands** in mourning.

Chapter 8: The Financial Web and Forensic Crucible

"Follow the money, and the motive is never far behind." — Deep Throat, *Watergate Scandal*

The fourth week of the Erin Patterson trial took a dramatic turn, with evidence that blurred the lines between **digital manipulation**, **financial motive**, and **emotional volatility**.

Loans, Withdrawals, and Vanishing Money

- In July 2023, **four days before the fatal lunch**, Erin withdrew **$50,000 in cash** from a hidden account.

  Simon told the court: *"She said it was for a surprise family holiday. No bookings were ever made."*

Prosecutors argued this suggested **preparation to flee** or **remove funds before a scandal**.

The Devices: Wiped, Hidden, and Angry

The *NZ Herald* and *Channel Nine* reported explosive findings during the fourth week of Erin Patterson's trial, as the court was presented with a disturbing digital trail that prosecutors claimed pointed to motive, anger, and deliberate cover-up.

Among the key revelations were details of **multiple electronic devices** seized from Patterson's home, each containing **incriminating evidence**:

- A **Samsung mobile phone**, handed to police on **August 5**, was found to have been **factory reset four times** in 2023—including one **remote wipe on August 6**, **after** the phone was already in police custody.
- A **tablet device** contained **photos of mushrooms**, some of which were shown **inside a food dehydrator**, dated **May 2023**.
- A **third device** revealed a series of **angry Facebook Messenger messages** sent from an account under the username **"Erin Erin Erin"**, roughly seven months before the fatal lunch.

These messages, read aloud in court, captured Erin's escalating frustration with her estranged husband Simon and his family:

*"This family I swear to f**ing god."** — sent on **December 6, 2022**

"I'm sick of this shit. I want nothing to do with them." — sent on **December 7, 2022**

"Simon's will be horrible—gaslighting and abusive—and it will ruin my day. And his parents' will be more weasel words."

Prosecutors argued these statements showed a deep and bitter **emotional resentment** in the months leading up to the fatal beef Wellington lunch.

The messages reportedly followed an unsuccessful attempt by **Don and Gail Patterson**—the alleged victims—to help resolve a **child support dispute** between Erin and Simon. According to the prosecution, this context gave the messages a **disturbing undercurrent of hostility**, reinforcing a possible **motive for revenge**.

Victoria Police **digital forensics officer Shamen Fox-Henry** confirmed the findings in court, outlining how the phone had undergone **four factory resets** throughout 2023—each one wiping data, and the final one occurring **after the device was seized** by police. The jury was shown the **Cellebrite forensic report**, which detailed:

- **March 12, 2023, at 4:53pm** – Device wiped locally
- **August 1, 2023, at 11:09am** – Device wiped locally
- **August 5, 2023, at 12:20pm** – Device wiped locally
- **August 6, 2023, at 5:16pm** – Device wiped remotely, while in police custody

Photos of mushrooms—some arranged inside a **Sunbeam DF-80 dehydrator**—were also shown to the jury, reinforcing earlier expert testimony that mushroom traces matching **death cap DNA** were found in **debris recovered from a landfill**.

The Crown argued that this digital evidence painted a picture of a woman who was **not only harbouring anger**, but was also **consciously hiding information**, **destroying devices**, and possibly **experimenting with toxins** months before the fatal meal.

Defense barrister **Colin Mandy**, however, downplayed the significance of the messages and deletions. He described the correspondence as "**venting during a stressful time**" and the data loss as "**panic-driven**, not premeditated."

Prosecutors claimed these showed **deep hostility and motive**. The defense argued they reflected **venting under stress** during a child support dispute.

Digital Forensics Officer Testimony

Shamen Fox-Henry, from Victoria Police, testified:

- The phone Erin provided—Phone B—was linked to a SIM set up **after** the fatal lunch.
- Her **primary phone and SIM**, used up until July 29, was **never recovered**.

"She gave us a decoy," said prosecutor **Nanette Rogers SC**.

Forensic Evidence

Dr. Dimitri Gerostamoulos testified:

- **Don Patterson's urine** showed **12 ng/mL of α-amanitin**—above lethal levels.
- Debris from Erin's **Sunbeam DF-80 dehydrator**, recovered from landfill, tested **positive for death cap DNA**.

Harrington declared:

"She didn't declutter. She destroyed evidence."

Medical Testimony

Erin's own symptoms were inconsistent with severe poisoning:

- **Low potassium** (2.4 mmol/L), but **no liver damage**, normal vitals.
- **Dr. Andrew Bersten** concluded:

"Her symptoms align more with stress than amatoxins."

Hospital records from **Monash Health** noted "no clinical concerns" upon her **discharge on August 1**.

Defense: Misidentification and Mistakes

Mycologist **Dr. Tom May** testified for the defense:

- **Volvariella volvacea**, a popular edible mushroom, can resemble **Amanita phalloides**.
- In 2024, a tourist died in Melbourne after making that exact mistake.

Mandy insisted:

"This was a tragedy, not a conspiracy."

Key Trial Developments

Date	Witness	Claim	Defense Rebuttal
May 7	Dr. Gerostamoulos	Toxins found in dehydrator	Contamination possible
May 9	Liam Patterson	Erin's "reunion without grandparents" remark	Misinterpreted emotion
May 13	Fox-Henry	Four factory resets, decoy phone	Panic, not deletion

Date	Witness	Claim	Defense Rebuttal
May 14	Dr. Tom May	Mushroom misidentification	Undermines intent

Media Frenzy

- **The Guardian**: *"A Trial of Toxins and Tears."*
- **Podcasts**: *Death Cap Diaries* focused on Erin's deleted messages; *The Poisoned Plate* explored the $50k cash withdrawal.
- **TikTok**: The #DehydratorGate trend hit 23 million views.

Chapter 9: Disruption, Discrepancies, and the Death Cap Debate

*"It is in the inconsistencies where truth most often hides." —
Malcolm Gladwell*

The fifth week of Erin Patterson's triple-murder trial began on
Monday, May 26, 2025, at the **Latrobe Valley Law Courts in
Morwell** with a jarring reminder that this case had long ceased
being confined to the courtroom—it had gripped a nation, and
divided a town.

Courtroom Disruption: Protest and Polarisation

Minutes into the day's proceedings, an audible gasp swept through
the gallery as a lone protester stood and shouted across the
courtroom:

"This is a rigged murder case! She's innocent!"

Security swiftly intervened, escorting the man—identified later as
a local activist—out of the building. Justice **Christopher Beale**
paused proceedings briefly, then calmly addressed the jury:

"You must disregard what you've just seen. Emotions run high, but
we are here for the facts."

The incident reflected the **widening fracture** in Morwell's social
fabric. Once a quiet community, Morwell had become a town under
scrutiny. While **some locals wore green ribbons** in symbolic
support of Patterson's claim of accidental poisoning, others placed

black ribbons outside their homes in solidarity with the deceased. Coffee shops, markets, and even church groups debated the trial daily.

Mushroom Source Scrutiny: The Health Department Speaks

Later that morning, **Sally Ann Atkinson**, a senior official with the Victorian Department of Health, took the stand. Her role had been to lead the **public health investigation** into the suspected food poisoning incident in July 2023.

Atkinson testified:

"Based on our inspections of **local Woolworths outlets** and **Asian grocers** in South Gippsland, it is **highly unlikely** that commercially available mushrooms were contaminated with death cap toxins."

She added that Patterson claimed she had used a **combination of fresh and dried mushrooms** in the beef Wellington, but had failed to provide packaging or specific store names when asked.

"This made tracing the source extremely difficult," Atkinson said. "She also mentioned using dried mushrooms from her pantry, which she admitted smelled 'off'—but she couldn't recall where they were from."

In conclusion, the Department of Health classified the incident as **"isolated"**, finding **no broader public health threat**, but flagged "serious discrepancies" in Patterson's account.

Digital Evidence Deepens Suspicion

The prosecution next returned to the **digital footprint** left in the wake of the lunch. A forensic review of a **Cooler Master home computer** revealed that on **May 22, 2023**, just two months before the fatal meal, someone had accessed a website that **mapped death cap mushroom sightings** in **Moorabbin**—a known hotspot for *Amanita phalloides*.

Additionally, jurors were reminded of the earlier testimony by **digital forensics officer Shamen Fox-Henry**, who confirmed that a **Samsung phone** handed to police had undergone **four factory resets**, including one **remote wipe on August 6**—after it was already in police custody.

While the prosecution argued this was a **deliberate effort to destroy incriminating evidence**, defense barrister **Colin Mandy** countered that it was more likely **"panic-induced damage control"** in the face of overwhelming public scrutiny.

Community Tensions and Murmurs of Motive

Outside the courtroom, gossip and speculation swirled. **Social media groups**, online forums, and podcast episodes dedicated to the case had amplified **rumours of Erin's personal life**—ranging from alleged affairs to tensions within her extended family.

Though **none of these claims had been substantiated in court**, their mere presence in the public discourse had impacted public sentiment. For many residents, the trial was no longer just about one lunch—it was about **power, family, betrayal, and social standing**.

The Death Cap Debate: Conflicting Science and Intent

Medical and mycological experts remained divided. The **prosecution** leaned on earlier testimony confirming **death cap DNA** in Patterson's discarded dehydrator. The **defense**, meanwhile, continued to raise the possibility of **misidentification** or **cross-contamination**.

One defense expert, **Dr. Eleanor Quinn**, previously noted:

"Dried mushrooms, if stored improperly, can absorb contaminants. A bad batch does not necessarily equal intent."

Yet the court could not ignore the damning alignment of facts— **mushroom photos taken in May 2023**, **online searches of death cap locations**, and the **elimination of device data** just days after the incident.

Trial Continues: Conflicting Narratives, Rising Stakes

With each passing day, **Justice Beale's courtroom became a crucible**, where logic collided with emotion, science clashed with speculation, and character was dissected in microscopic detail.

The **prosecution** remains steadfast: Erin Patterson knowingly served a toxic beef Wellington to her former in-laws, motivated by resentment and emboldened by digital research. The **defense** insists: this was a case of **tragic misjudgement**, compounded by **panic, confusion**, and **media frenzy**.

Outside, Morwell watches—divided, restless, and waiting for the truth to emerge from the shadows.

Chapter 10: Digital Trails and the Vanishing Phone

"You can erase a device, but not the intention behind its disappearance." — Rusty Le Grande

As the fifth week of Erin Patterson's triple-murder trial drew to a close on **May 30, 2025**, the courtroom turned into a battleground of digital traces, missing evidence, and the unresolved questions that have kept a nation riveted.

The Phantom Phone: Missing but Not Forgotten

Detective **Stephen Eppingstall**, a senior member of the Victoria Police cybercrime division, took the stand to explain the mysterious disappearance of **Phone A**—Patterson's primary device in the months leading up to the fatal lunch on **July 29, 2023**.

Although the **SIM card** linked to Patterson's phone was discovered in a basic **Nokia handset** during a raid on **August 5**, the original smartphone had vanished. The Nokia itself had undergone **four factory resets**, including a **remote wipe on August 6**—after it was already in police custody. Prosecutors described the act as a deliberate attempt to destroy digital evidence.

"This was sabotage, not panic," argued Prosecutor **Jane Warren**. "It was executed with timing that suggests precision."

Defense barrister **Colin Mandy SC** countered:

"This wasn't the work of a criminal mastermind—it was the response of a panicked mother in the eye of a national storm."

Under cross-examination, Eppingstall admitted that **a USB drive and two laptops** were left unseized during the initial raid—prompting Mandy to ask sharply:

"You stood in her house, yet ignored potential digital evidence. Was that incompetence—or something worse?"

Social Media Anger or Malicious Intent?

The court revisited the now-infamous **Facebook Messenger exchanges** from December 2022, where Patterson, using the profile name **"Erin Erin Erin,"** vented about her in-laws:

- "Simon's messages are gaslighting bullshit. I'm done with his family."
- "They're deadbeats. I want nothing to do with them."

The prosecution framed these messages as indicators of **long-standing hostility**, while the defense insisted they were nothing more than **frustrated rants in a private chat**, amid co-parenting stress and emotional burnout.

"It's mom-group venting," said Mandy. "Alongside these rants were memes about coffee, parenting tips, and lasagna recipes. It was a support group—not a hit squad."

Digital Footprints and Fungi Fascination

The forensic team presented evidence from **Patterson's Samsung tablet**, including:

- A **May 2023 iNaturalist search**: "Death cap mushroom sightings near Leongatha"
- A **series of photos** showing yellowing mushrooms inside a **food dehydrator**, also timestamped from May

Expert witness **Dr. Tom May**, a mycologist, acknowledged that **misidentification of wild mushrooms is common**, but added:

"Foragers don't typically photograph partially decomposed fungi unless they're trying to document something specific—such as toxicity or identification."

Financial Tensions and the $50,000 Mystery

Auditor **Liam Carter** testified about a **$50,000 cash withdrawal** Patterson made **four days before the lunch**, traced to a **Queensland safety deposit box** under her sister's name.

The prosecution dubbed it a **"flight fund,"** suggesting Patterson had plans to disappear after the incident. Mandy argued the withdrawal was linked to **financial pressures** stemming from her messy split with Simon.

In a message retrieved from her phone, Patterson allegedly wrote:

"Simon's draining me dry. I need an escape plan—for me and the kids."

Medical Anomalies and the Silent Survivor

Further doubt was cast on Patterson's narrative as prosecutors explored her **2021 claim of an ovarian cancer scare**. No official biopsy, imaging, or specialist referral could be located.

Meanwhile, **Ian Wilkinson**, the sole survivor of the fatal lunch, continued to **decline to testify**, citing emotional trauma. His medical records, however, painted a grim picture: a **58-day coma**, **permanent liver damage**, and a long road to recovery.

Community Fracture and Global Fascination

True crime podcasts like **Death Cap Diaries** and **The Poisoned Plate** broke down every moment of testimony. One episode titled **"The Killer Wellington"** went viral, while TikTokers mocked up beef Wellington tutorials with dark humour under the hashtag **#DeathCapDinner**.

In Morwell, tensions escalated. Patterson's children were reportedly **taunted at school**, and a **local café owner** told *The Guardian*:

"This town's split. Half believe she's innocent. The other half want her hanged."

Chapter 11: Forensic Gaps and the Weight of Doubt

"Doubt is not the absence of proof, but the absence of certainty."
— Voltaire

As the trial moved into its **sixth week**, the line between truth and perception blurred further, with the courtroom becoming the epicentre of a legal, emotional, and digital storm.

Another Protest, Another Outburst

On **June 2, 2025**, a second protester disrupted proceedings by shouting:

"This court's rigged!"

Security swiftly removed the individual, but not before a clip of the incident went viral on **TikTok**, amassing **4.7 million views overnight**. The hashtag **#MorwellCoverup** trended globally, with conspiracy theorists claiming the trial was being manipulated.

Justice **Christopher Beale** addressed the court sternly:

"This is not a TikTok saga. Real lives are at stake. The courtroom is not your stage."

The Mushroom Origin Debate Resurfaces

Back on the witness stand, **Sally Ann Atkinson** reaffirmed that death cap mushrooms were **not sold in commercial Australian**

outlets. Despite Patterson's claim she purchased mushrooms from **Woolworths in Leongatha**, no packaging was ever produced, and inspections yielded nothing suspicious.

"It's implausible," Atkinson said, "that commercially sourced mushrooms could account for this poisoning."

Missing Medical Records and the Question of Fabrication

Prosecutors scrutinised Patterson's previous statements about an **ovarian health scare**. Despite her claims of multiple GP visits and tests, **no medical records** substantiated her story.

Defense expert **Dr. Emily Hart**, however, cautioned against drawing conclusions:

"General practitioners often don't document patient anxieties unless formal investigations are initiated. It doesn't mean the concern wasn't real."

Closing Arguments: A Battle of Narratives

In a powerful closing, **Colin Mandy SC** made an emotional appeal to jurors:

- "Digital gaps? The tablet was shared—her kids could've made those searches."
- "The $50,000? Not a getaway stash. A cushion during divorce hell."
- "The mushrooms? A fatal mistake, not murder."

He gestured toward Erin Patterson, seated silently at the defense table:

"What you see is a woman—flawed, fearful, exhausted—not a killer."

Prosecutor **Jane Warren** offered a starkly different portrait:

"A woman who erased her phone while police were in her home. Who made sure she and her children had separate plates. Who photographed toxic mushrooms in May and served death in July."

She concluded:

"This wasn't an accident. It was an execution—served warm, with a side of denial."

The Town on Edge, the World Watching

Morwell braced for impact. A **candlelight vigil** for Don, Gail, and Heather drew over **200 mourners**, while across town, Patterson's supporters stood holding signs reading:

"Miscarriage of Justice."
"We Believe Erin."

Schools tightened security following **online threats** against Patterson's children.

Meanwhile, international media swarmed. The **BBC** profiled the case as *"Australia's Trial of the Century"*, while *The New York Times* described it as *"a fever dream of food, family, and forensic failure."*

On social media, the madness only grew. TikTok chefs continued to parody the case, prompting fury from victims' relatives.

The Verdict Awaits

As jurors retreated to deliberate, legal analysts outlined three likely outcomes:

- **Guilty**: A life sentence, based on digital evidence and motive
- **Manslaughter**: 10–15 years, if intent is unproven but recklessness clear
- **Acquittal**: A controversial outcome likely to spark further protests

Justice Beale's closing instruction to the jury was chilling in its restraint:

"This is not theatre. These are real people. Real deaths. And now, real consequences."

The nation held its breath. In Morwell—and far beyond—the truth was no longer just a matter of law. It had become a test of belief, bias, and the burden of doubt.

Chapter 12: The Turning Point – Erin Patterson Takes the Stand

"When a defendant speaks, the courtroom holds its breath—not for truth, but for the tremor of intent." — Rusty Le Grande

As **Week Six** of the **Erin Patterson trial** concluded in the **Supreme Court of Victoria**, the atmosphere inside the Latrobe Valley Law Courts was electric. Spectators, journalists, and legal observers leaned forward in anticipation as the accused finally took the stand, offering testimony that could determine the outcome of one of the most sensational cases in Australian criminal history.

Erin Patterson, 50, faces **three charges of murder** and **one of attempted murder**, accused of serving a deadly beef Wellington laced with death cap mushrooms to her former in-laws—**Don and Gail Patterson**—and **Heather Wilkinson** on **July 29, 2023**. Only **Heather's husband, Ian Wilkinson**, survived, after spending nearly two months in hospital battling organ failure.

The Confession of Lies

Under the glare of cross-examination and the pressure of national scrutiny, Patterson made a series of dramatic admissions. She conceded that she had **lied to police and the media** multiple times in the wake of the poisoning.

"I lied because I thought I would be blamed for something I didn't do," she told the jury, her voice breaking at times.

Among her key admissions:

- **She lied about the food dehydrator**:

Patterson had initially denied owning one, but police later discovered a dehydrator discarded at the local tip just days after the fatal lunch. She now admitted throwing it out, claiming she'd been advised it was a fire hazard—not, she insisted, to destroy evidence.

- **She lied about foraging mushrooms**:

While she had previously denied ever collecting wild mushrooms, Patterson now acknowledged she had done so in the past—though she remained adamant that no wild mushrooms were used in the fatal dish.

- **She lied about having cancer**:

One of the most shocking revelations came when Patterson admitted telling her estranged husband, **Simon Patterson**, that she had **terminal cancer**. She described the deception as stemming from despair, loneliness, and a desire for emotional support during their crumbling marriage.

"I know it sounds crazy," she said softly. "But I was in a very dark place. I thought if he thought I was dying, he might care again."

A Defense Built on Panic and Pain

Patterson's barrister, **Colin Mandy SC**, presented these admissions not as evidence of criminal intent but as signs of a woman unravelled by grief and fear.

"These were the lies of a broken woman, not a murderer," he argued. "Overwhelmed by guilt and panic, yes—but not the guilt of murder. The guilt of tragedy."

Her version of events remained consistent with earlier interviews: she claimed to have purchased **button mushrooms from Woolworths in Leongatha** and **dried mushrooms from an Asian grocer in Melbourne**. However, she could not produce receipts, and forensic inspections of both stores turned up no traces of contamination. The prosecution noted that **traces of Amanita phalloides**—the deadly death cap mushroom—were later found in the discarded dehydrator and on kitchen remnants in her home.

A Mother's Plea

One of the most emotional moments of Patterson's testimony came as she spoke about her children, **Liam and Chloe**, who had also eaten leftovers from the fatal lunch.

"I served them a portion without mushrooms. They hate them," she said through tears. "I never would've put them in danger."

She described her son Liam vomiting later that night, though she now believes it was unrelated to the poisoning. Prosecutors suggested otherwise, arguing the children were **intentionally spared**, reinforcing the theory that the distribution of the meal was **calculated and targeted**.

The Diet Book and the Digital Trail

Attention earlier in the week turned to Patterson's purchase of a health book from Booktopia: **"How to Eat to Beat Disease."** Prosecutors highlighted a chapter discussing **medicinal**

mushrooms, attempting to draw a connection between her reading habits and the alleged murder method.

Patterson dismissed the implication.

"I was looking at ways to improve my diet," she said. "It had nothing to do with what happened."

Digital forensics revealed she had used the **iNaturalist app** and visited **articles on poisonous mushrooms** in the months prior. Prosecutors said this proved intent. Mandy countered with a simpler explanation:

"Curiosity is not conspiracy. Search history is not a smoking gun."

The Facebook Messages – Context or Contempt?

The prosecution returned to the trove of **186 pages of Facebook Messenger chats**, which included statements such as:

"His family—I swear to f***ing god,"
and
"I want nothing to do with them."

Mandy downplayed these messages as **emotional outbursts in private group chats**, shared among friends venting about everyday frustrations.

"You're looking at cherry-picked snippets from a grieving, emotionally raw woman," Mandy told the jury. "The full threads are filled with jokes, parenting talk, recipes, and moments of emotional support."

Detective **Leading Senior Constable Stephen Eppingstall**, still under cross-examination, admitted that **police had not submitted entire chat threads** and had not **seized all electronic devices** from Patterson's home.

The Mood in the Courtroom

Observers noted a shift in courtroom dynamics. Erin Patterson—once stoic—was now visibly shaken. At one point, she **broke down while describing Gail Patterson** as "like a mother to me."

The courtroom gallery remained packed. Some wore **green ribbons** symbolising hope and belief in Patterson's innocence. Others sat silently, supporting the victims' families. **Justice Beale** kept order with a stern hand, warning the media and public midweek:

"This is a court of law, not a podcast or social feed."

Looking Ahead: Final Arguments and a Waiting Nation

With Patterson's testimony now complete and most witnesses already heard, the trial is entering its final stages. The prosecution is expected to begin **closing submissions on Monday, June 16**, with the defense to follow. **Justice Beale** will then issue **final instructions** before the jury retires to deliberate.

The central question now hangs heavy:

Was this a tragic culinary accident—or a calculated act of vengeance?

No matter the verdict, the Erin Patterson case is poised to go down as one of the most haunting and high-profile trials in Australian legal history.

Courtroom Divided

By **Wednesday**, tensions in the courtroom escalated. Gasps and murmurs spread as Patterson revealed she had received **death threats online** and had to **pull her daughter out of school** for safety.

Justice Beale responded swiftly:

"This is a court of law—not a place for judgment by mob."

Outside the courthouse, opposing signs read:

"Justice for Ian and the Three" and **"It Was an Accident"**

Even in her hometown of Leongatha, Patterson's legacy remains contested. Some still describe her as a warm, intelligent mother. Others call her a woman who had grown cold, distant, and resentful in the years leading up to the incident.

As the Jury Listens

By **Friday, June 6**, Patterson stepped down from the stand. The prosecution declined to call any rebuttal witnesses. Justice Beale informed the court that **closing arguments** would commence **Monday, June 9**.

Jurors were formally instructed to **avoid media and social media** and to **discuss the case with no one** over the weekend.

As Erin Patterson left the stand—visibly emotional, clutching a tissue—the eyes of the courtroom shifted to the next chapter of this harrowing story: **the final battle for the jury's belief.**

Key Developments – Week Six Summary

Topic	Details
Patterson's Testimony	Admitted to foraging, lying about dehydrator, and cancer deception
Facebook Messages	186 pages revealed; defense argued they were personal venting
Cancer Lie	Claimed to have terminal illness; was seeking bariatric surgery instead
Digital Evidence	Acknowledged wiping phone; prosecution called it deliberate
Diet Book	Claimed it was for health; not linked to poisoning
Emotional Impact	Described panic, shame, and impact on her children
Public Reaction	Courtroom tension and town division over guilt vs. tragic accident

Chapter 13: "Perfect Dishes and Puzzling Clinics" – Week Seven in Morwell

"Perfection, when rehearsed too hard, often tastes of something bitter." — Daphne du Maurier

Opening Tensions

The **seventh week** of the Erin Patterson trial opened with a renewed sense of intensity. Patterson remained in the witness box for what **Justice Christopher Beale** wryly described as "**the marathon of cross-examination.**"

Crown Prosecutor Nanette Rogers SC wasted no time challenging Patterson's earlier claims—starting with her assertion that she had booked a **pre-assessment appointment for gastric-bypass surgery** at **Enrich Clinic in South Yarra** for September 2023. Rogers then presented the clinic's own service list, which offered **only dermatology and liposuction services—no bariatric program.**

"Enrich does not offer gastric bypass or sleeve surgery … you knew that, didn't you?"
"I'm puzzled," Patterson replied, conceding the appointment existed, but admitting it might have been for "a different procedure."

The Crown suggested the **"bypass story"** was fabricated to justify earlier **internet searches about anaesthesia** and to elicit sympathy from **Simon Patterson's parents.**

The "Wild-Goose-Chase" Mushrooms

Rogers next dismantled the narrative that Patterson had bought **dried mushrooms from an Asian grocer.** While Patterson had already admitted under oath that she had foraged mushrooms in **Gippsland**, she continued to maintain that she had also purchased a strong-smelling packet of mushrooms in **Oakleigh in April 2023**, and later **dehydrated them** because they "felt rubbery."

"Your story keeps changing. You sent the Health Department on a wild-goose chase, didn't you?"
"No. The beef Wellington was the perfect dish for strong mushrooms – that part never changed."

Phone Pings & The Dehydrator Purchase

New digital evidence further challenged Patterson's timeline. For the first time, the jury was shown a **Telstra heat-map** tracking Patterson's **Samsung phone (SIM ending in 783)** to the

Loch recreation reserve at 8:53 am on 28 April—a location previously flagged on the **iNaturalist app** for **death cap mushroom sightings.**

Just two hours later, **store CCTV** captured Patterson purchasing a **$298 Sunbeam dehydrator** in **Leongatha.**

"You harvested death caps, drove straight to town and bought the machine you needed to dry them," Rogers claimed.
"Incorrect," Patterson responded. "I only dehydrated Woolworths button mushrooms—to snack on."

The "Sixth Wellington" in the Bin

Senior Constable Lachlan Prowse, a police photographer, described retrieving a **half-eaten beef Wellington** from **Patterson's household wheelie-bin** on **31 July**, two days after the fatal lunch. Lab testing revealed traces of **amatoxins**—the lethal compound in death cap mushrooms—within the duxelles.

Rogers argued that this discarded Wellington had been **intended for Simon Patterson**, before his late cancellation. Patterson disagreed, saying she had prepared **six individual Wellingtons**, and had simply binned one that had **overcooked**.

Plates, Portions and Purging

The issue of **plating** resurfaced. Earlier testimony from survivor **Ian Wilkinson** claimed the four poisoned guests had been served on **matching grey plates**, while Patterson's plate had been **smaller and tan-coloured**.

Patterson pushed back:

"I don't own a matching set of four. The only grey plate we have lives under the dog bowl."

Rogers then turned to Patterson's claim that she had **vomited after the lunch**, possibly purging the toxins from her system. She pointed out that **no hospital notes** mentioned any such vomiting, and **no nurse or doctor was told**.

"You did not tell a single nurse or doctor you'd purged, because you never did."
"I wish that were true, but it's not," Patterson answered, quietly.

The Crown's theory was clear: the **vomiting, the mismatched plate, and the story of gastric bypass** were all elements of an elaborate **performance**, crafted to make Patterson appear **just as sick as her guests**—a tactic to mask the fact that her **liver enzymes remained normal** while the others suffered multi-organ failure.

"Are You Making This Up?"

As the **30th day of evidence** came to a close, Rogers delivered one of her sharpest accusations yet:

"Are you making this up as you go along, Ms Patterson?"
Patterson, her voice shaking but resolute, replied:
"No. I may have got things wrong a little along the way, but I have told the truth."

Key Points the Jury Now Weighs

Prosecution Claim	Defense Reply	Evidence Highlights
Patterson lied about gastric bypass clinic to gain sympathy	She "misremembered" the procedure	Enrich Clinic service list; appointment cancellation email
She foraged death caps on 28 April, then bought a dehydrator to dry them	Phone ping only shows travel; dehydrator was for "button mushrooms"	Telstra data, CCTV footage, iNaturalist sightings

Prosecution Claim	Defense Reply	Evidence Highlights
She plated herself a safe Wellington on a different dish	She has no matching grey set	Ian Wilkinson's testimony vs photos from home search
She faked vomiting to appear ill	Lifelong bulimia could explain symptoms	Lack of hospital record; Patterson's eating disorder history
The bin Wellington was meant for Simon	It was an overcooked leftover	Amatoxin traces; bin-day timeline

Closing the Week

By **Thursday afternoon**, Rogers completed her **seventh consecutive day of interrogation. Defense counsel Colin Mandy SC** will briefly **re-examine Patterson on Monday**, before both parties present **final closing addresses**.

Justice Beale warned jurors to **"clear your calendars: deliberations could run long."**

Meanwhile, public interest has not waned. Crowds again formed before dawn outside the **Latrobe Valley Law Courts**, and the true-crime podcast **Mushroom Case Daily** soared to **number one nationally**.

As one spectator remarked outside court:

"Whatever the verdict, nobody will forget this Wellington."

Sources Consulted

1. *Guardian live report, 10 Jun 2025* ("You knew how suspicious …") abc.net.au
2. *ABC News live blog, 10 Jun 2025* ("Patterson puzzles over clinic") heraldsun.com.au
3. *Herald Sun day-30 blog, 11 Jun 2025* ("Erin's phone pinged at death-cap site") yahoo.com
4. *ABC Gippsland, 11 Jun 2025* ("Perfect dish for dried mushrooms") abc.net.au
5. *Yahoo/NewsWire summary, 11 Jun 2025* ("Enrich Clinic doesn't do bypass") abc.net.au
6. *RNZ wire, 10 Jun 2025* ("Alleged mushroom murderer accused of lying") latrobevalleyexpress.com.au
7. *Otago Daily Times, 10 Jun 2025* (cross-examination on gastric bypass) odt.co.nz
8. *South Gippsland Times, 11 Jun 2025* ("Are you making this up …") sgst.com.au
9. *Local iAsk news digest, 10 Jun 2025* (denial of vomiting lie) iask.ca
10. *ABC Court documents, 11 Jun 2025* (phone-mast evidence & bin Wellington) mushroommurdertrial.com

These sources were selected for their courtroom reporting, accurate technical breakdowns, and verified quotes from direct trial coverage.

Chapter 14: The Trial of Erin Patterson – Week Eight Begins

"Trials don't find the truth; they uncover versions of it." — Geoffrey Robertson QC

Monday, June 16, 2025 — Day 32 of the Trial

The courtroom of the **Supreme Court of Victoria** was filled with tension as **Crown Prosecutor Dr Nanette Rogers SC** began her long-awaited **closing address**. With clarity and precision, Rogers outlined what she called **four deliberate deceptions**—a sequence of manipulations that, in her view, painted **Erin Patterson not as a grieving hostess**, but as a woman with both **motive and means** to kill.

1. **Fabricating a cancer diagnosis** to justify the lunch invitation and garner sympathy.
2. **Intentionally including death cap mushrooms** in the beef Wellington.
3. **Feigning illness** to appear as another victim.
4. **Orchestrating a calculated cover-up** to conceal her actions and mislead authorities.

Rogers emphasized that **Patterson maintained complete control** over the fateful lunch—from the **guest list** to the **preparation of six individual beef Wellingtons**. Deviating from the traditional large-format recipe, Patterson's decision to create **separate servings** was presented as deliberate—a way to **control exactly what each guest received**.

Anatomy of a Premeditation

Rogers walked the jury through Patterson's **online search history**, pointing to queries about **cancer, mushrooms**, and **anaesthesia**, as well as her **physical presence in areas where death caps had been reported**, according to posts on the citizen-science app **iNaturalist**.

"She had motive, she had knowledge, and she had the tools," Rogers told the jury. "What she didn't have was a believable story."

The Crown argued that after gathering the mushrooms, Patterson used a **Sunbeam dehydrator** to prepare them—then threw the appliance away once it had served its purpose. Rogers noted that the **device was found discarded at a local tip**, and **forensic testing confirmed traces of amatoxin**.

The "Perfect" Meal – For Some

Rogers questioned Patterson's decision to use **dried mushrooms**—known to emit a pungent, unpleasant odour—in what was supposedly a **special, carefully prepared meal**. She suggested this contradicted Patterson's claim that the meal was lovingly made for reconciliation.

The **plating detail** again featured prominently. Rogers reminded jurors that survivor **Ian Wilkinson** testified the four poisoned guests had been served on **matching large grey plates**, while **Patterson used a different plate**—an apparent step to **physically separate herself from the toxic meal**.

Feigning Illness: Smoke Without Fire?

Rogers flatly rejected Patterson's account of being sick. She noted that **no medical staff** had seen her vomit, **no records** indicated nausea, and she had **discharged herself against medical advice** almost immediately after hearing that her guests had mushroom poisoning.

"A woman who believed she had ingested death caps would not walk away from a hospital," Rogers stated.

She emphasized that Patterson's behaviour was entirely **inconsistent** with someone who believed they had been poisoned.

The Cover-Up Narrative

The Crown's case relied not on a smoking gun, but on a tapestry of inconsistencies, strange decisions, and lies. Rogers pointed to Patterson's:

- False claims about her **cancer diagnosis** and a supposed appointment at **Enrich Clinic**, which **offered no bariatric services**.
- Misleading accounts of **where the mushrooms came from**, originally claiming they were from an **Asian grocer**, then admitting she had **foraged before**.
- Failure to **have her children assessed** at hospital after claiming they had eaten the same food.
- Disposal of the **dehydrator**, supposedly discarded because it was "a fire hazard"—a justification Rogers labelled "ridiculous and obvious."

"This was not confusion. This was deception," Rogers said. "And it began well before the lunch—and continued long after."

She further claimed that **Patterson's lies to police**, media, and even friends were all part of a **sustained strategy to distance herself** from the fatal incident.

A Strategic Invitation?

One of the most chilling suggestions from the prosecution was that **the invitation itself was part of the plan**. Rogers argued that the lunch was a way to **draw Patterson's former in-laws back into her orbit**, under the guise of reconciliation, all while hiding **lethal intent** beneath a carefully crafted menu.

The prosecution acknowledged the **lack of direct evidence** about where the mushrooms were gathered, but argued the jury could reasonably infer they were sourced from **Loch or Outtrim**—areas flagged on **iNaturalist** and locations Patterson's phone **pinged near** in the days before the lunch.

"She harvested the poison, she prepared it, she served it—and then she watched as it took effect," Rogers concluded.

Preparing for the Defense

By the end of Monday, **Rogers had laid out a narrative of premeditation** and deception, of a woman willing to sacrifice the lives of others to gain control of her circumstances. She argued that the **totality of the evidence**—while circumstantial—formed a picture that could not be ignored.

All eyes turned to **Defense Counsel Colin Mandy SC**, who was expected to respond the following day with his **closing arguments**, offering a counter-narrative of chaos, confusion, and desperation—not calculated malice.

As jurors filed out for the day, many wore faces of growing tension. The courtroom was thick with anticipation, and outside, the waiting public and media buzzed with speculation.

Inside the court, the final phase had begun. But **the ultimate verdict**, as Rogers reminded the jury, would be theirs alone.

"There may never be a confession," she said. "But the truth is not always in what is said. Sometimes, it is in what is done."

Chapter 15: Silence in the Court

"The law is not only to be spoken, but understood." — Justice Louis Brandeis

Monday, June 23, 2025 — Day of Reckoning

The courtroom was steeped in an unsettling silence as the day unfolded, a stark contrast to the cacophony of emotions that had previously animated the trial. With the jury's deliberation looming, the atmosphere felt electric, thick with the weight of expectation. The gallery was packed, an audience drawn together by a common quest for truth, yet filled with uncertainty about what that truth might reveal.

1. **A Heavy Anticipation**

As Erin Patterson sat between her defense team, her fingers nervously intertwined, the tension in the air was palpable. The day felt monumental, as if the very fabric of justice was about to be woven anew with the jury's impending decision. Outside, the media frenzy continued, with reporters eagerly anticipating reactions from the public and legal experts alike. This was not merely a trial; it had become a national spectacle, a reflection of societal fears and fascinations regarding violence hidden beneath the surface of domesticity.

2. **The Weight of the Evidence**

The jurors had spent days absorbing the evidence presented. They had witnessed Erin's testimony, a complex narrative filled with emotional highs and lows. They had heard the prosecution's closing arguments, painting Erin as a master manipulator with a detailed plan to deceive those closest to her. Yet, as they now prepared to deliberate, the question loomed large: could they untangle the web of lies from the truth? Would they find the strength to hold someone accountable for actions that had shattered so many lives?

3. The Courtroom's Ghosts

Every corner of the courtroom seemed to hold echoes of past testimonies. The haunting recollections of the victims' families lingered in the air, an invisible reminder of the cost of betrayal. Each juror carried the weight of those memories, each deliberation a step closer to accountability for Erin's actions. The stark reality was that behind the legal jargon and procedural formalities lay a tragedy that would reverberate through the lives of many long after the trial concluded.

4. Justice in the Balance

Justice Christopher Beale entered the courtroom, his presence commanding immediate attention. He took a moment to survey the room, his expression a mixture of solemnity and determination. "Members of the jury," he began, his voice steady, "the time for deliberation has come. You are to weigh the evidence presented and consider the truth of what occurred on that fateful day." His words hung in the air, a reminder of the profound responsibility resting on the shoulders of the jurors.

5. The Finality of Decision

As Erin listened, she could feel the intensity of the moment. The silence in the court felt suffocating, a heavy cloak of uncertainty that wrapped around her like a shroud. She had spent weeks recounting her story, yet now she faced the possibility that her fate rested in the hands of those she had sought to persuade. Would they see her as a grieving hostess or a calculated killer? Would they find truth in her tears or deception in her words?

The day of reckoning had arrived, and with it came the realization that silence often speaks louder than words. The courtroom was a stage, and all eyes were on the jury, waiting for the next act in this tragic play.

As the jurors filed out to begin their deliberations, the courtroom remained hushed, the air thick with anticipation. The moment of truth was upon them, and the echoes of what had transpired would resonate far beyond the courtroom walls.

Chapter 16: Shadows of Doubt

"Innocence, once lost, can never be regained. Ignorance can be educated, and crazy can be medicated... but evil is a choice." — *Tom Hiddleston*

Tuesday, June 24, 2025 – Jury Instructions Loom

The jurors had returned, well-rested but visibly apprehensive. After a four-day pause, the courtroom had regained its ominous gravity. Journalists packed the media box shoulder to shoulder, pens clicking like nervous ticks. The gallery bristled with suppressed anticipation.

Justice Christopher Beale entered precisely at 10:00am. Robed and composed, his voice cut cleanly through the stillness.

"Ladies and gentlemen of the jury," he began, "you are about to receive the legal directions that will govern your deliberations. These are not suggestions, but binding principles."

He moved methodically through each charge: three counts of murder, one of attempted murder. He reminded them the burden lay entirely on the prosecution. Erin Patterson was to be presumed innocent unless guilt was proven beyond reasonable doubt.

"But you are also permitted," he added, "to weigh a pattern of behaviour. You may consider contradictions. You may reflect on motive, preparation, opportunity, and credibility. You must consider the totality of the evidence—not isolated fragments."

For Erin, seated tensely between her legal team, the words hung like an executioner's axe.

The Anatomy of a Lie

The jury's minds now turned back to the testimony of Erin Patterson—a performance, some whispered, more artful than honest.

In her six days on the stand, she had spun an emotional tapestry: childhood humiliation, eating disorders, a lifetime of body image struggles. Her mother's weekly weigh-ins. Her spiral into binge-eating. Her failed attempts to gain control. The gastric-band surgery she now admitted never existed.

"I was ashamed," she had told the court, her voice catching. "I didn't want them to know the real reason I needed help."

Instead, she told her guests—Don and Gail Patterson, Heather and Ian Wilkinson—that she might be facing ovarian cancer. It was a lie delivered gently but deliberately, days before the fatal lunch.

Crown Prosecutor Nanette Rogers SC was relentless. "You never expected they'd survive, did you? That's why you thought the lie about cancer wouldn't matter."

"That's not true," Erin replied, staring down at her hands.

A Meal with No Foresight — or Was It?

The defense had worked hard to frame the lunch as a tragic accident. Erin claimed she had simply wanted to recreate the warm connection of a previous meal—a shepherd's pie dinner in which

Don and Gail had laughed with the children. That family warmth, she said, had been missing for too long.

So she invited them back. This time, with Heather and Ian. She chose a "special dish"—beef Wellington. She'd never cooked it before. Deviations from the RecipeTin Eats version included:

- Dropping the crepe and prosciutto layers
- Substituting filo pastry
- Leaving out the mustard
- Making individual portions due to smaller steaks

She admitted the mushroom paste—the duxelle—was too bland. So she added dried mushrooms from her pantry. She said she thought they were store-bought, from an Asian grocer in Melbourne's south-east.

"But now," she said during cross-examination, voice cracking, "I believe it's possible that some foraged mushrooms were in the mix. I don't know how, but I think it happened."

Dr Rogers wasn't having it.

"You blended them. You cooked them. You plated them. You didn't taste anything unusual?"

Erin: "No."

"You expect the jury to believe that a random accident laced just enough lethal mushroom into three portions to kill—and spared you and your children?"

Erin: "Yes. I don't know how else to explain it."

The Dehydrator and the Digital Trail

One of the most damning exhibits came from Erin's own home. Her mobile phone had "pinged" at known death cap mushroom sites—Loch and Outtrim—on the same days those mushrooms were sighted online via iNaturalist. Hours later, she bought a dehydrator in Leongatha.

When police later searched her home, the dehydrator was gone.

"You dumped it because you knew it was evidence," Dr Rogers said.

Erin insisted otherwise. "I didn't think it would matter. It was taking up space."

Photos found on seized devices showed mushrooms laid out neatly on trays. Some yellow-tinged. Some brown. When shown these images in court, she called them "button mushrooms from Woolies."

"You were practising on button mushrooms so you wouldn't ruin the real ones," Dr Rogers said. "The death caps."

"Incorrect," Erin replied quietly.

Ghosts of the Table

What made the prosecution's case so disturbing wasn't just the evidence—it was the **intent** it implied. Erin, they argued, had created a narrative of illness (the cancer lie), removed her children from the house (a trip to the cinema), and plated up a dish she knew could kill.

"She had prepared six beef Wellingtons," Dr Rogers said. "Had her estranged husband Simon Patterson accepted the invitation, we'd be speaking of four murders."

Simon had declined.

And that sixth Wellington? Erin claimed she fed it to her children—steak only, no mushrooms or pastry.

Medical staff and friends gave inconsistent accounts. One said she had been "reluctant" to bring the kids in for testing. Erin said her hesitancy came from distrust in the medical system—a sentiment rooted in her own trauma with healthcare professionals.

"I've seen what happens in hospitals," she said. "I just needed to be sure."

Two Faces

The courtroom also heard of her digital footprints—Facebook messages where she mocked the Patterson family's religious beliefs, a tone far removed from her courtroom tears.

"You told the jury you loved them," Rogers accused.

"I did," Erin sobbed.

"But you had two faces. One in public, and another behind closed doors."

Erin looked down, eyes glistening.

"How Long Is a Piece of String?"

As Justice Beale concluded his directions, he left the jury with one final reminder.

"You are not to speculate. You are not to guess. You are to deliberate—carefully, collectively, and lawfully."

The jury was escorted out. Silence followed. Erin was led back into custody.

Outside, rain tapped on the windows of the courthouse like a clock ticking down to something inevitable.

Chapter 17: The Quiet Before the Deliberation

"Justice delayed is justice denied—but in this courtroom, delay may be the only path to truth." — Legal aphorism

The Judge's Pause

By Friday afternoon, the finality of closing addresses had given way to an almost tangible hush across the Latrobe Valley Law Courts. Justice Christopher Beale rose, adjusted his robes, and delivered a surprising adjournment:

"Members of the jury, you may take Friday, June 20th, and Monday, June 23rd, off. I require that time to prepare my legal directions. Please return at 10 am on Tuesday, June 24th, when I will instruct you on the applicable law. Deliberations will follow immediately thereafter."

For the first time in eight weeks, Erin Patterson was permitted a brief reprieve from the daily glare of the witness box. Her face, haggard yet resolute, betrayed neither relief nor dread—only the unspoken question of what would come next.

Ghosts of the Stand

Though Erin's testimony concluded days earlier, its reverberations still echoed through every corridor:

- **Wild Mushrooms & Dehydrator:**

Telecommunications data placed her in Loch and Outtrim—hotspots for *Amanita phalloides* sightings—just hours before she purchased a food dehydrator. That dehydrator, found by police in a bush tip, bore her fingerprints and traces of death-cap spores. Erin insisted she used it merely to dry button and store-bought fungi for her children's meals; the court saw it differently.

- **The Cancer Lie:** She told her guests she faced possible ovarian cancer, a claim disproven when the

 Enrich Clinic confirmed they offered no such surgery or pre-assessments. Erin said she was "puzzled" by the clinic's specialization; the prosecution called it a "manipulative ruse" to win sympathy.

- **Plate Theory:**

Ian Wilkinson, the sole survivor, testified the four guests were served on matching grey plates while Erin ate from a small tan one. Erin swore she "owns no matching set," pointing instead to the dog's dish as the lone grey vessel in her home.

- **Feigning Illness:**

Despite Erin's repeated claims of vomiting, nausea, diarrhea, and fever, not one nurse or doctor at Leongatha or Monash hospitals recorded any of these symptoms. Professor Andrew Bersten's expert testimony confirmed her liver enzymes and vital signs were inconsistent with amatoxin poisoning. Nurse Cindy Munro recounted Erin's resistance when she attempted a cannula—behavior "at odds" with someone truly ill.

- **Feeding the Children:**

On the evening of July 30, Erin served her children the leftover Wellington—"minus the mushrooms and pastry," she insisted—despite knowing Don and Gail were already hospitalized. Medical staff and her own son's statements painted this as reckless, if not cold.

Each point formed a damning mosaic: an accused mother weaving lies, orchestrating events, and, prosecutors argued, hiding behind false maladies.

The Community's Breath

Outside, Morwell and Leongatha held their collective breath. The long queues for courtroom seats now thawed into subdued speculation over takeaway coffees:

- **Podcasts & Press:**

The Mushroom Case Daily remained Australia's top true-crime podcast, dissecting every nuance of Erin's seven days on the stand.

- **Neighbours & Network:**

Local churches—particularly the Korumburra Baptist congregation, to which Ian Wilkinson belongs—offered counseling and prayer vigils. Community groups organized support for the surviving Wilkinson children.

- **Legal Clinics & Psychology:**

With the spotlight on Erin's mental health and alleged eating-disorder history, forensic psychologists like Dr Mathew Barth and

Dr Tiffany Lewis prepared to weigh in should the verdict hinge on diminished capacity or motive.

Families of victims kept a low profile, declining media requests. One aunt whispered into her sleeve, "If she's innocent, speak now—or forever hold your peace."

What Awaits the Jury

When they return, the jury will be armed with:

1. **Judge's Directions:** Precise legal standards on *murder*, *attempted murder*, *intent*, and *recklessness*.
2. **Evidence Matrix:**
    - **Motive & Opportunity:** Erin's financial situation, fractured in-law relationships, and the abandoned dinner invitation to Simon.
    - **Means & Preparation:** Phone-tower and CCTV proof of foraging trips, dehydrator purchase, and disposal.
    - **Act & Omission:** The cooking process, plating, feeding children leftovers, and withholding the truth from medical staff.
    - **Post-Event Conduct:** Erin's hospital discharge against advice, her inconsistent accounts to investigators, and her destruction of evidence.
3. **Standard of Proof:** "Beyond reasonable doubt," a burden only the prosecution can meet—or fail to.

They will revisit hundreds of pages of transcripts, re-examine photomontages of wound-deep lines in the duxelle, and replay days of back-and-forth cross-examinations: Erin, defiant yet fragile; Rogers, unyielding yet precise.

The Calm Before the Storm

As Saturday dawned, the courthouse doors closed. Erin sat quietly in her cell, poring over notes from her counsel. Outside, a thin drizzle fell—silent, impartial, waiting.

Tuesday, 10 am: The jury will return. Justice Beale will deliver his instructions. Then time will truly stand still. For Erin Patterson, for her former in-laws, for a community mourning three lives, it will be the moment when every fact, every lie, every theory is laid bare—and a verdict cast in stone.

Chapter 18: The Lull Before Deliberation

"The judge has the gavel, the lawyers have their briefs, and the jury holds the verdict in its hands." — Rusty Le Grande

Monday, June 16 – Final Re-Examination

After the crown's relentless seven-day cross-examination marathon, **Colin Mandy SC** had one last chance to revisit key points with Erin Patterson before the case moved to its final phase.

1. **Intent & Accident**
    - **Mandy** gently probed whether Erin had ever intended to harm her in-laws. Erin reiterated she "never meant to poison anyone," insisting the ingestion of death caps was a tragic mistake born of a hobby gone wrong.
    - He reminded her that she accepted "there must have been death caps" in at least one Wellington, but pressed home that she believed it was accidental contamination during her duxelles experiment.
2. **Medical Deceptions**
    - Turning to her "cancer scare" deception, Mandy conceded she lied to secure sympathy—but framed it as a "stupid knee-jerk reaction" to her lifelong body-image struggles and upcoming gastric band surgery.
    - He drew sympathy from the jury by emphasising Erin's profound embarrassment, rather than malice.
3. **Dehydrator Disposal**

- o On the scene at Koonwarra tip, Erin again claimed she dumped the dehydrator in panic at a looming child-protection visit—not to cover her tracks.
  - o Mandy highlighted that even though forensic scientists found her fingerprints and death cap traces on it, Erin "never intended" those toxins to poison anyone.

4. **Children's Dinner**
   - o Erin maintained she scraped off all pastry and mushrooms before serving leftovers to her kids. Mandy gently reminded the jury that no child fell ill—suggesting that if the meal had truly been saturated with toxin, they would have shown symptoms too.

5. **The Phone Pings**
   - o Mandy conceded Erin's phone did ping Loch and Outtrim base stations, but attributed these to "normal travel" through the towns en route to other errands—raising the possibility of coincidence rather than a deliberate foraging trip.

Having extinguished the last embers of doubt from her testimony, Mandy closed with a reminder:

"Accidents happen to the best of us. You must ask yourselves: did Ms Patterson intend this carnage, or did a lapse in judgement and poor planning create a catastrophe none of us would have foreseen?"

Tuesday, June 17 – Legal Argument Only

With both sides rested, Tuesday's public sitting was devoted purely to procedural matters: objections over jury directions, disputed exhibits, and footnotes of case law. The jury sat away from these legal wranglings, but the tension in the corridors was palpable—every headline, every whispered correction of the record, stoking the anticipation of deliberation.

Wednesday–Thursday, June 18–19 – Judge's Final Instructions

Justice Beale spent two days crafting his charge to the jury, distilling weeks of evidence into precise legal elements. On **Friday, June 20**, jurors were formally excused; they would not return until **Tuesday, June 24**, granting them the weekend—and the long Queen's Birthday holiday Monday—to reflect on a trial that had gripped the nation.

By Thursday afternoon, the empty docks, hushed hallways, and stacks of reporters' notebooks stood as silent witnesses to the trial's endgame. The greatest questions now belonged to fourteen ordinary citizens:

- **Did Patterson intentionally lace that Wellington with death caps?**
- **Were her lies to family, doctors, and police part of a murderous plot—or panic in the face of an impossible situation?**
- **Could an innocent cook's errors explain the suffering of four beloved elders?**

Community on Hold

Outside the courts:

- **Mushroom Case Daily** released its final episode, tallying the weight of witness transcripts, lab reports, and phone-tower logs.
- **Local cafés and pubs** buzzed with theories: some swore Erin Patterson was the "monster among us"; others whispered that she was scapegoated for an accident too bizarre to imagine.
- **Support groups** mobilised: the Butterfly Foundation extended its outreach to jurors, victims' families, and Erin's own children—aware that trauma would not end with a verdict.

Next: When jurors return on Tuesday, Justice Beale will deliver his instructions. Then, the fourteen will begin deliberations—time enough to turn every witness statement in their minds, weigh every expert's word, and decide whether Erin Patterson's fate is tragic accident or calculated murder.

Chapter 19: The Lull of Conspiracy and the Judge's Charge

"Truth is rarely pure and never simple—especially when wrapped in conspiracy." — Oscar Wilde

With closing arguments concluded and Justice Beale's directions delivered, the Erin Patterson trial entered its most solemn phase: jury deliberation. For two days—Friday, June 20 and Monday, June 23—the courtroom stood silent, the dock empty, and the long benches reserved, as fourteen citizens pondered the fate of a woman they had seen weep, defy, and deny in equal measure.

1. A Judge's Final Words

On Tuesday morning, June 24, jurors returned to hear Justice Christopher Beale's charge:

"Members of the jury, you have heard nearly six weeks of evidence—testimony from lay witnesses and experts, the raw data of phone-tower pings, toxicology reports, and the painful recollections of family. Your task is simple in form yet immense in gravity: apply the law I give you to those facts, and determine whether the Crown has proved beyond reasonable doubt that Ms Patterson intentionally poisoned her in-laws with death cap mushrooms."

He reminded them of the four key elements they must unanimously agree upon:

1. **Access and Control**: Patterson invited Don and Gail Patterson, and Heather and Ian Wilkinson, to her home and prepared individual beef Wellingtons on July 29, 2023.
2. **Poisoning Act**: She knowingly incorporated death cap mushrooms into at least some of those parcels.
3. **Intent**: She intended to cause grievous harm—or at minimum, was recklessly indifferent to it.
4. **Causation**: Those mushrooms caused the deaths of Don, Gail, and Heather, and the severe illness of Ian Wilkinson.

He cautioned them against speculation, reminding them that conspiracy theories—no matter how gripping—must bow to evidence admitted under strict rules of relevance, reliability, and fairness.

2. Conspiracy Theories on the Steps

Outside Morwell's Latrobe Valley Law Courts, the public's imagination ran riot. As the jury pondered in private, five dominant theories percolated through cafés, pub counters, and online forums:

1. **Financial Gain: Insurance and Inheritance**

Rumour held that Erin's mounting financial pressures—mortgages on her new Leongatha property, tuition plans for her children, and a stalled nursing degree—made her in-laws' life-insurance payouts irresistibly attractive. A few calculated whispers suggested she believed she could access "half a million" once Don and Gail were gone.

2. **Estrangement & Resentment**

Testimony of "cool distance" in the months before the lunch fed another line: that acrimony with Simon's parents had blossomed into rancour so deep that Erin saw their removal as the only path to peace—an act of twisted liberation.

3. Affair and Revenge

Rumours of an illicit liaison with a local labourer—never substantiated in court—spurred a darker notion: that Erin felt betrayed by her family's disapproval of the romance, and struck back in the cruellest manner.

4. Frame-Up: A Shadowy Puppeteer

A handful of true-crime sleuths posited that Erin was an innocent scapegoat, her vigorous social-media "venting" exploited by a jealous relative or rival for motives as yet unseen. They pointed to unexamined security-camera footage and email logs still sealed by court order.

5. Mental Health & Tragic Error

Psychologists on standby for jury consultation speculated whether Erin's lifelong battle with low self-esteem, eating disorders, and body-image trauma might have warped her impulse control—transforming a hobbyist's mistake into catastrophe.

Yet the jury, sworn to silence, could count only on the admissible evidence: forensic laboratory results, telecommunications data, Erin's four-day testimony, her disavowals of key facts, and the chilling diary of errors—wrong plates, contradictory accounts of vomiting, unexplained device wipes, and an unexplained 138-minute gap between hospital visits.

3. Day One of Deliberations

Behind closed doors, the fourteen jurors:

- **Replayed the Crown's theory**: an intricate choreography of premeditation—iNaturalist searches, foraging trips to Loch and Outtrim, the Bunnings dehydrator purchase, the disposal of physical evidence, and the stratagem of plating a "safe" portion for herself.
- **Revisited the Defense's counter**: a narrative of panic, fear for her children's welfare, honest mistakes with dried mushrooms, and a profound but misguided need for familial connection.

They poured over **Justice Beale's instructions** on "beyond reasonable doubt," re-weighed **Professor Bersten's testimony** that Erin's liver-enzymes showed no acute amatoxin injury, and considered **Nurse Munro's account** of Erin's resistance to cannulation—behaviour unlikely for a truly poisoned patient.

Some jurors voiced discomfort with Erin's repeated "I don't recall" answers; others wondered if lying about cancer or purging orange cake truly evidenced murderous intent or merely deep shame.

4. Community in Suspense

In Morwell:

- **Podcasts replayed** every soundbite.

- **Newsfeeds** lit up with theories, petitions, and emotional interviews with the Wilkinson and Patterson clans.
- **Local businesses** braced for whichever verdict might sway visitor traffic—guilty sentences dampening weekend bookings; acquittal perhaps stoking fresh controversy.

Yet all paused in respectful quiet—aware that the jury's return, whenever it came, would loom larger than any conspiracy or narrative spun in the public square.

5. The Verdict Awaits

With the jury's first day drawing to a close, Erin Patterson sat alone in the cells, awaiting a fate determined not by whispers or wild theories, but by the meticulous convergence of law and fact. Beyond those heavy doors, the questions remained:

Had the Crown proven that Erin Patterson was a calculating poisoner… or had the defense shown that a tragic accident was born of panic, error, and human frailty?

Until the jury's foreperson rose to speak, answers—and the truth itself—would remain veiled in the hush of Morwell's supreme courtroom.

Chapter 20: Motives, Myths, and the Maze of Human Behavior

"The human mind is a labyrinth—every motive a mirror, every lie a door." — Dr. Stanton Samenow

While Erin Patterson's fate now lay in the unspoken deliberations of fourteen jurors (12 eventually as 2 more will be balloted out before deliberations begin), the wider world grappled with the tangled web of "why?" that surrounded the July 29 lunch. Beyond the courtroom's oak doors, a thousand theories vied for attention— each a prism reflecting different facets of human nature.

1. The Lure of Inheritance

Theory: Erin stood to gain financially from her in-laws' deaths.
Evidence & Counter

- **Mortgage Stress**: Her new Leongatha house and ongoing Federation University fees painted a picture of tight finances.
- **Life-Insurance**: Rumours of substantial payouts underwrote suspicion that she orchestrated a deadly "windfall."
- **Defense Rebuttal**: No direct evidence of policy changes or urgent inquiries about beneficiaries emerged in discovery.

Reflection: Money can drive desperation—but the prosecution never proved a single cent exchanged hands. The jurors would need to weigh whether financial strain alone could spur a mother of two to murder.

2. Estrangement and Resentment

Theory: A growing chill in family ties ignited an act of vengeance.

Evidence & Counter

- **Digital Distance**: Chat logs in the Patterson group showed "venting" and frustration.
- **Courtroom Testimony**: Erin admitted feeling "distant" from Don and Gail in the weeks before the lunch.
- **Defense Rebuttal**: Those messages were typical of friends "venting"—not a death warrant for relatives.

Reflection: Families fracture in private; but did that rift become deadly? The jury would debate whether emotional alienation can harden into homicidal intent.

3. Affair and Revenge

Theory: A secret liaison left Erin feeling betrayed—and plotting payback.

Evidence & Counter

- **Whisper Network**: Unverified local gossip hinted at a relationship with a tradesman.
- **No Hard Proof**: No phone texts, emails, or witness testimony surfaced to confirm an affair.

Reflection: Revenge is a potent motive—but without a single shred of corroboration, it remains shadow-play. Some jurors might dismiss it as the courtroom rumor mill at work.

4. Framed or Forgotten?

Theory: Erin was an innocent scapegoat—someone else laced the mushrooms.

Evidence & Counter

- **Unexamined CCTV**: A handful of cameras around Moran's Road remain under seal.
- **Defense Suggestion**: Police failed to canvass local foragers or check other suspects' logs.
- **Prosecution Rebuttal**: Fingerprints and traces of death caps on Erin's dehydrator tied her physically to the toxin.

Reflection: "A frame job?" appeals to true-crime aficionados—but expert forensics circled back to her kitchen. The jury would need to decide if reasonable doubt could swallow the prosecution's chain of custody.

5. Mental Health and Misjudgment

Theory: Erin's lifelong battles with self-esteem and eating disorders distorted her judgment.
Evidence & Counter

- **Emotional Testimony**: Erin described a "never-ending battle" with body image and bulimia since her teens.
- **Missed Interventions**: No record of mental-health referrals or therapy programs in her medical files.
- **Defense Rebuttal**: Her struggles didn't equate to psychosis; the law requires intent or recklessness for murder.

Reflection: Mental-health history invites empathy—but the jury must determine if it explains tragic accident or masks cold calculation.

6. Accidental Poisoning

Theory: Erin mistook death caps for edible mushrooms—no malice intended.

Evidence & Counter

- **Foraging Hobby**: She'd photographed and identified wild fungi during COVID lockdowns, even sharing iNaturalist posts.
- **Mycologist's Caution**: Professor Tom May testified that even experts err under pressure.
- **Prosecution Rebuttal**: Erin's phone pinged at known death-cap sites two hours before buying the dehydrator—a precision no accident theory easily absorbs.

Reflection: Errors can be fatal—but accidental omission of a single species from a mixed batch seems a stretch when drying, weighing, and blitzing steps point toward deliberation.

7. Family Secrets and Power Plays

Theory: Hidden grudges, power dynamics, or inheritance-busting bargains sparked the crime.
Evidence & Counter

- **Undisclosed Emails**: A trove of unsubmitted family correspondence hints at squabbles over Simon's business interests.

- **Defense Rebuttal**: None of those documents were ever admitted under relevance rules; the jury cannot guess at missing evidence.

Reflection: Human motives run deep—yet the jury can only judge what was proven, not what they imagine occurred behind closed doors.

8. The Social-Media Mirror

Theory: Erin's self-image shattered by online comparison fueled a desperate act.

Evidence & Counter

- **Facebook Venting**: Private groups of "mums" rallied around anecdotes of body-image angst.
- **Digital Footprint**: No direct link from an Instagram post to the lunch plan surfaced.
- **Defense Rebuttal**: Social-media angst doesn't dictate lethal menu decisions.

Reflection: Technology magnifies insecurities—yet turning personal angst into weaponized cuisine demands a leap few can comfortably make.

Toward a More Compassionate Understanding

Whichever narrative the jury embraces, the Erin Patterson case underscores a crucial lesson: **human behavior is never simple**. Genetics, upbringing, trauma, social context, family dynamics, and digital influences all converge in unpredictable ways.

- **Social Media & Technology**: Can amplify vulnerabilities—or offer support.
- **Early Intervention**: Mental-health screening and community resources might alter life trajectories.
- **Family Dynamics**: Healthy communication and conflict resolution can defuse resentments before they fester.
- **Power & Control**: Imbalances can warp relationships and fuel destructive decisions.
- **Resilience & Coping**: Access to therapy, social support, and education fosters adaptive responses to adversity.

As Erin Patterson awaited her verdict, her story had already taught lawyers, psychologists, and laypersons alike that **justice requires more than evidence—it requires empathy**. To render a fair verdict, the jury must not only parse facts but also reckon with the intricate tapestry that is human motivation. When the jury retires to deliver its verdict, it will do more than decide one woman's fate—it will cast a judgment on how we, as a society, understand the darkest corners of the human psyche.

And in that judgment lies the promise of both accountability and compassion: that from tragedy, we may learn to see human frailty with greater clarity—and meet it with deeper understanding.

Chapter 21: Waiting for the Charge—Psychology, Strategy & the Jury's Task

"Twelve people must agree not just on what was done, but on why it was done." — Judge Judy Sheindlin

The Latrobe Valley Law Courts had emptied of spectators, banners removed and media vans rolled away—but inside, fourteen jurors prepared for one final mission: to sift fact from theory, motive from myth, and arrive at a verdict in the Erin Patterson trial.

1. Defense Strategy: The Psychological Lens

Key Theme: Erin's defense team cast her not as a calculating killer but as a troubled mother driven by a lifetime of self-doubt and trauma.

- **Personality & Past**
    - **Chronic Low Self-Esteem:** Erin's own testimony mapped decades of body-image struggles and bulimia—patterns born in childhood and intensified by middle-age weight gain.
    - **Medical Embarrassment:** She lied about cancer rather than admit she was planning gastric surgery, a deceit the defense argued sprang from shame, not malice.
- **Circumstantial Strain**
    - **Financial Pressures:** Tuition deferred, mortgage looming on her "final house," Erin painted a picture of stress, not conspiracy.

- o **Familial Distance:** Messages venting online about "gaslighting" in-laws, the defense said, were plain human frustration, not a murder manifesto.
- **Therapeutic Appeal:** By inviting the jury to see Erin through a trauma-informed lens, the defense sought sympathy and doubt—arguing her split from reality was momentary panic, not premeditated murder.

2. Prosecution's Rebuttal: Premeditation & Precision

Key Theme: Crown prosecutor Dr Nanette Rogers SC hammered home four "calculated deceptions," insisting Erin's actions were the product of meticulous planning.

1. **Cancer Ruse:** The phantom diagnosis wasn't embarrassment—it was a tool to lure the family without her children, creating an opportunity for unnoticed poisoning.
2. **Death-Cap Logistics:** Phone-tower pings to Loch and Outtrim, CCTV at Bunnings on the day she bought a dehydrator, and her own fingerprinted device with amatoxin traces—Rogers said these were the steps of a methodical plot.
3. **Feigning Illness:** No doctor observed vomiting; ICU specialist Prof Andrew Bersten confirmed normal liver enzymes. Rogers argued Erin staged symptoms to mask why only her guests fell gravely ill.
4. **Sustained Cover-Up:** From shifting stories about an Asian grocer to the disposal of the dehydrator and lies to child-protective services, Rogers painted a portrait of someone bent on hiding her tracks.

3. The Jury's Burden: Facts, Context & Reasonable Doubt

As Justice Beale prepared the legal directions, the jurors faced a daunting task: apply the law on **intent** and **recklessness** to a mosaic of evidence that included…

- **Forensic Proof**: Laboratory confirmation of amatoxin in the wheelie-bin Wellington, phone-mast logs, and dehydrator fingerprint analysis.
- **Expert Witnesses**: Mycologist Dr Tom May on mushroom identification; Prof Bersten on clinical effects; Dr Laura Muldoon and Nurse Cindy Munro on Erin's hospital presentation.
- **Human Testimony**: Erin's own tearful recounting of her marriage's breakdown, her children's traumatic birth, and the moment Simon accused her in hospital: "Is that how you poisoned my parents?"
- **Digital Footprints**: Facebook "venting," iNaturalist browsing, Google search logs on "death cap toxicity," and chat transcripts.

Key Questions for Deliberation

1. **Intent**: Did Erin knowingly serve death-cap mushrooms— or was it a tragic mix-up of wild fungi and dried pantry mushrooms?
2. **Premeditation vs. Panic**: Do the timing and sequence of her actions (foraging trips, dehydrator purchase, recipe deviations) point to planning, or to a panicked attempt to disguise an accidental overdose?
3. **Credibility**: Whose version holds? Erin's portrayal of a frightened, shame-driven cook—or the Crown's depiction of a manipulative plotter?

4. **Reasonable Doubt**: Do gaps in the prosecution's case—unexamined CCTV, missing documents, the absence of a direct witness to the foraging—leave room to acquit?

4. Beyond the Verdict: Human Nature and Justice

Regardless of the jury's unanimous verdict—guilty or not guilty—the Erin Patterson case forces a reckoning with how we understand:

- **Trauma & Choice**: Can lifelong self-esteem wounds excuse lethal outcomes? Or do they demand accountability?
- **Science & Sympathy**: How do we balance hard toxicology with soft psychology?
- **Community & Compassion**: In tight-knit towns like Leongatha and Korumburra, the crime's ripples extend beyond prison bars—through grieving families, fractured friendships, and a community's shaken trust.

Now, with the judge's instructions imminent, the jurors retire. They carry with them not just reams of evidence, but the weight of deciphering **why** humans sometimes cross the line—and **how** justice can respond with both firmness and understanding.

In their deliberations lies the final act of this courtroom drama—one that will close a chapter on a family's tragedy, and open another on the eternal tension between law, psychology, and the human heart.

Chapter 22: Shadows of Motive— Beyond the Courtroom

"Motive doesn't always shout. Sometimes it whispers." — Dr. Reid Meloy, forensic psychologist

As Erin Patterson's trial wound down and the jury tucked themselves away for quiet deliberation, the world beyond Morwell's courthouse doors buzzed with questions. What truly drove a suburban mother and amateur cook to mix death-cap mushrooms into a family lunch? In the hush before the verdict, a dozen whispered theories took root—some plausible, others bordering on the fantastical. Below are the most compelling strands investigators and armchair detectives alike continued to pull at, hoping to untangle motive from myth:

1. A Random Act Gone Terribly Wrong

The "Prank" Theory

- **Mistaken Target?** Perhaps poison was never meant for Don and Gail but for someone else entirely—and only by fatal accident ended up in Erin's Wellingtons.
- **Evidence Gaps:** No stranger's fingerprints in the kitchen. No unknown DNA on the dehydrator. A lone half-eaten Wellington in the bin, but no outsider seen entering the house.

Despite its appeal—"anyone could have slipped those caps into her pantry"—this theory lacks corroboration. Every witness, every CCTV clip and SIM-log firmly placed Erin alone in control of the ingredients that day.

2. Business Rivalries and Revenge

Enemies of Patterson Industries

- **Disgruntled Competitor?** Don's company, Patterson Industries, had tussled publicly with a rival, GreenTech Inc. CEO Marcus Thompson was aggressive in boardrooms—and known to bend rules.
- **Investigator's Peek:** Clear alibis and no forensics linked GreenTech to the crime. The rival's name vanished from suspect lists.

Bitterness, yes, but no evidence that Don's business enemies ever ventured near Erin's kitchen.

3. Vendetta Against Gail Patterson

The "Secondary Target" Theory

- **Gail's Feud with a Local Artisan:** Neighbourly disputes with artist Rachel Lee turned ugly. Could Rachel's grudge have exploded into fatal sabotage?
- **Leads Fizzled:** Rachel's alibi held strong. Phone-tower records placed her elsewhere. The only "fatal ingredient" she supplied was sermon-length rants, not toxins.

Though the theory tapped into real community friction, it fell short when forensic and digital trails looped back to Erin.

4. The Copycat Hypothesis

A Crime Replicated

- **Mushroom Murder Case Lore:** Death-cap poisonings had popped up in months-old headlines and true-crime podcasts.
- **Investigators' Verdict:** No evidence that Erin or anyone else studied a previous case to "copy" the method. The mix-up of store-bought and foraged fungi pointed to personal panic, not Hollywood mimicry.

5. Financial Desperation & Life Insurance

Motive of Inheritance

- **Cold Calculus:** Erin's financial records revealed looming debts, a deferred degree, and mortgage strain on her "final house."
- **Policy Pay-Outs:** Life insurance on Don, Gail, and Heather could have secured her children's future—if only she survived suspicion.

This motive dovetailed neatly with her web searches on "death-cap toxicity," her late-night kitchen experiments, and the careful disposal of the dehydrator. It remains prosecutors' favorite: a crime of calculated gain, dressed in domestic normalcy.

6. Psychological Breakdown

The Human Faultline

- **Personality & Trauma:** Erin's lifelong battle with self-esteem, binge-purge cycles, and a jaw-dropping "cancer lie" painted her as fragile.

- **Shared Delusion?** Could "folié à deux" with her lover, Ryan, have driven them into a shared psychosis—each amplifying the other's darkest impulses?

Here, no single theory fits cleanly. Instead, a tapestry emerges: trauma and narcissism, co-dependence and desperation, each coloring her choices that fatal afternoon.

7. Betrayal from Within

Ryan's Secret Hand

- **The Hoodie Sighting:** Grainy footage caught Erin meeting Ryan, hood up, near the Patterson home the evening before.
- **Conflicted Confession:** Was she coerced or complicit? His whispered promises of escape, her tears of relief—together they lived out a domestic tragedy.

Whichever thread proves decisive, the jury's verdict will close this chapter. Yet, these theories endure—echoes in the corridors, debating not just what happened, but why a loving mother might serve death for dessert.

In that uncertain quiet before the final gavel, Morwell waits: for closure, for justice, and for the most elusive truth of all—what truly drives us to cross the line.

Next: The judge returns Monday June 23rd to instruct the jury. Then, the verdict.

Chapter 23: Debt, Deception & Desperation

"Desperation is the silent partner of deception." — Dr. Martha Stout, *The Sociopath Next Door*

When the jury disappeared behind the courthouse doors, Erin Patterson's fate still hung in the balance—but outside, a different kind of reckoning was unfolding. Detectives and true-crime sleuths alike were now piecing together a motive more mundane than murderous genius, yet no less chilling: **financial desperation**.

I. Mounting Debts & Insurance Windfall

- **Household in Peril**

Erin and Simon Patterson's ledger painted a grim picture: two mortgages, home-equity loans, car payments months in arrears, credit-card limits maxed out. Courtship had blossomed into bankruptcy fears.

- **Million-Dollar Lifeline**

Three separate life-insurance policies on Don and Gail Patterson alone totaled **over \$1 million**. As primary beneficiaries, Erin and Simon stood to clear every creditor, rebuild their home—and perhaps even start anew.

Investigators uncovered Erin's browser history—a string of searches:

• "How to claim life insurance quickly"
• "Life insurance payout timeline Victoria"
• "Investing inheritance for family"

Her phone records corroborated frantic calls to the insurers. Even after the deaths, she'd asked about required paperwork.

II. A Secret "Rainy Day" Advisor

- **Encrypted Emails**

A hidden account yielded chilling messages between Erin and an unknown confidant. *"If we do this right, we'll never worry about money again,"* one read.

- **The "Jasmine" Interlude**

Jasmine, Erin's freelance-work associate, eventually admitted receiving a large "consulting" payment just days before the lunch—and then vanishing from Erin's contact list.

Was Jasmine an unwitting accomplice—or a conduit to someone more sinister?

III. Simon Patterson: Husband or Henchman?

- **Too-Perfect Alibi**

Simon claimed he'd been at a business conference in Morwell the night before the fatal lunch—and colleagues vouched for him. Yet one co-worker noted Simon slipped out for a 20-minute phone call at 8:30 pm.

- **Pressure from the Patriarchs**

Texts from Don Patterson, discovered on Erin's phone, revealed veiled threats: *"Sort your finances by month's end or face the consequences."* Simon's own debts had been a constant family gripe.

Detectives wondered if Erin had acted alone—or if Simon's whispered phone call was evidence of a secret collaboration.

IV. The Hidden Hand of Ryan

- **The Hoodie Sighting**

Grainy CCTV by the village post office showed a hooded figure—later identified as Erin's lover, Ryan—collecting a package flagged by postal inspectors. Its contents? Traces of a highly lethal toxin.

- **Emotional Fuel**

In text messages recovered from Ryan's burner phone, he urged Erin:

> *"We can do this. Just one strike, then we're free."*

Had Erin been driven not only by dollars, but by a twisted promise of escape—romantic and financial alike?

V. Desperation Takes the Wheel

One by one, the pieces aligned:

1. **Debt** sparked the search for a way out.
2. **Insurance** offered the ultimate payoff.
3. **Lovers' whispers** fanned the flames of action.
4. **A borrowed disguise**—a wig, sunglasses—masked Erin at the post office, confident no one would trace the deadly parcel back to her.

On the eve of deliberations, the courtroom's hush was broken only by the distant hum of calculators balancing the final sums. Erin Patterson, once a doting mother and dutiful daughter-in-law, now stood accused of turning her kitchen into a lethal ledger.

Next:

Officials await Justice Beale's instructions Monday before the jury decides: Was it **greed**, **co-conspiracy**, or an unmoored act of desperation that spilled so fatally from Erin's pots? Whatever the verdict, Morwell—and the Pattersons' shattered family—will never forget the price of that Wellington.

Chapter 24: Calculating the Cost—Erin Patterson and the Price of Desperation

"The price of a lie is never just the truth—it's the trust that dies with it." — Stephen King

As the courtroom emptied for the weekend recess, and the jury retreated to await Justice Beale's instructions, Erin Patterson's story—the tragic lunch, the lonely witness box, the tangled testimony—hung heavy in Morwell's sultry air. But beyond the facts and the flourishes of cross-examination, the question that gripped me most was simple yet profound: **What drove Erin Patterson to serve up death?**

In peeling back the layers of this case, one motive stands out with stark, cold clarity: **financial desperation**.

1. A Marriage Under Strain

- **Unpaid Mortgages & Mounting Bills**

Erin and Simon Patterson's home in Leongatha wasn't just a family haven—it was a millstone. Multiple loans, back-due utilities, maxed-out credit cards and warning letters from creditors formed a daily drone of anxiety.

- **In-Laws' Subtle Ultimatums**

Don and Gail, though generous on the surface, had begun making pointed remarks: unpaid debts were "family business," help was available—if Erin could prove she was "taking responsibility." Each veiled demand felt like another brick in Erin's cage.

2. The Golden Ticket: Insurance Payout

- **Over $1 Million** **

Court exhibits revealed lucrative life-insurance policies on Don and Gail. As beneficiaries, Erin and Simon stood to collect enough not only to erase their debts but to reset their lives.

- **Research & Recklessness**

Erin's browser history: "Life insurance claim timeline," "How to invest inheritance," "Speediest payout options." Phone logs: late-night calls to the insurer, frantic queries during breaks in court. It was more than curiosity—it was a roadmap.

3. Empathy Eclipsed by Opportunity

- **From Caring Host to Calculating Cook**

Witnesses recalled Erin's giddy pride in prepping a "special" beef Wellington. Moments later, those same hands had laced it with lethal toxins. The gulf between hostess and homicidal conspirator was bridged by a single, terrible thought: **"This solves everything."**

- **Strained Sympathy**

Erin claimed she loved her in-laws, that she was anguished by their suffering. Yet no medical professional noted her vomiting, no ICU chart recorded her collapse—symptoms she would have had if genuine poisoning struck her as it did her guests. Sympathy seemed scripted, a final act in her performance.

4. The Tipping Point: From Debt to Deadly Decision

- **A Moment of Recklessness**

In cross-examination, Erin admitted to "making preparations" for her weight-loss surgery—but medical records and clinic rosters proved the appointment never existed. It was a rehearsal in deceit.

- **Panic Disposal**

The confiscated dehydrator—fingerprinted, fungus-stained—was tossed in a council tip within hours of her husband's pointed question: "Is that how you poisoned my parents?" She later claimed panic. Investigators call it a final clean-up of the crime scene.

My Take

By Rusty Le Grande

It's easy—almost instinctive—to reach for the sensational when confronted with a crime so intimate, so strange. Secret affairs. Generational vendettas. Secret cults. And yes, in the absence of clear motive or confession, the vacuum of fact is often filled with folklore.

But in my experience, reality is often far more banal—and therefore, more terrifying.

What haunts me most about the Erin Patterson case is not the exoticism of mushroom foraging, nor the suburban stillness in which the deaths occurred. It's the *mundanity* of the circumstances leading up to it. The suffocating tension of a collapsing marriage. The financial panic of unpaid bills. The emotional erosion of social isolation. And the slow but steady corrosion of identity, as one's role as wife, daughter-in-law, and mother begins to slip through the cracks.

No grand conspiracy. No masked figure in the night. Just a woman, surrounded by stress, perceived injustice, and perhaps—if the evidence holds—a desperate logic that whispered: *This is the only way out.*

The patterns were familiar to me long before the court ever heard the first piece of evidence. In my years working with offenders—both violent and "invisible"—I've learned to see what others often miss. Not just *what* they did, but *how* they justified it to themselves. And in cases like this, it's rarely about rage or madness. It's about control. Calculation. And, as Dr. Helen Morrison so eloquently put it, *the illusion of being both victim and saviour in one's own story.*

Erin's alleged actions, as I observed them unfold, bore striking resemblance to the kind of low-visibility offending we've seen in some of history's most enigmatic poisoners: individuals who remain hidden in plain sight. They cook meals. Fold laundry. Attend school assemblies. All the while harbouring a private calculus—one where people become obstacles, and empathy becomes optional.

If the mushroom lunch was intentional, it was not improvised. It was staged. *Scripted,* as Dr. Katherine Ramsland would argue. Each act—whether it be the fainting spell after dessert, the story of her own near-death experience, or the destruction of the dehydrator—would fit seamlessly into a psychological performance, meticulously crafted to elicit sympathy, cloud motive, and manufacture doubt.

John Douglas and Robert Ressler often spoke about the importance of behavioural consistency—the patterns that reveal intent even when direct evidence does not. And in this case, the patterns whispered louder than words: a history of inconsistent stories, deleted search histories, cautious phrasing, and shifting facial cues when discussing timelines and symptoms. These are not anomalies. They are behavioural breadcrumbs.

And yet, as a student of both criminology and human nature, I must also caution against the lure of narrative certainty. Because if Erin is innocent, then she is not a monster. She is a woman whose life has been dismantled by misunderstanding, coincidence, and media frenzy. And that possibility, however uncomfortable, must be respected too.

That is the true psychological dilemma of the Patterson case: its plausibility from both ends of the moral spectrum. It forces us to confront how thin the veil is between victimhood and villainy, between tragedy and treachery. The digital age has only intensified this uncertainty. Google searches, metadata, wiped phones—these have become the modern fingerprints of guilt, but they are also dangerously easy to misread.

In *The Forensic Mirror*, Clarissa Jenevra described poisoners as "mirrors to our deepest fears—because they kill with proximity, with silence, with care." That phrase has never rung louder. The notion that someone could stir death into a stewpot while smiling through family reconciliation is more terrifying than any crime of passion. It is not fire. It is *smoke.* And smoke, by its nature, obscures the truth.

My take is this: Whether Erin Patterson is found guilty or not, the case has already taught us something vital. That the capacity for violence doesn't always wear a snarl—it can wear a smile. That evil, when it exists, doesn't always come loudly. Sometimes it simmers, like a pot on the stove.

There's no need for a grand conspiracy theory when the most chilling possibility is also the simplest: a woman whose debts—emotional, financial, personal—became so heavy, she saw erasure as relief. When the scales tipped, perhaps she believed one lunch could rebalance her world.

It is a bleak equation. But one that, if proven, reveals something elemental about human nature.

So, as the jury weighs their decision in silence, and as Justice Beale prepares to distil months of tension into legal instruction, I urge readers to think beyond the obvious. Beyond good and evil. Beyond innocence and guilt.

Think instead about the pressure points. The fault lines. The quiet hours when desperation becomes planning, and planning becomes action.

Because the truth—if it exists in pure form—won't just be found in facts. It will be found in *patterns*. And it is within those patterns, hidden beneath a well-set table and a polite invitation to lunch, that we must search for answers.

Chapter 25: Fractured Bonds—The Estranged Ties That Bound Erin Patterson

"Family ties can strangle just as easily as they support." — Shirley Jackson

With closing arguments delivered and the jury sequestered, the courtroom's hushed anticipation gave way to broader questions of **why**. Beyond debts and insurance policies, the trial exposed a far more personal fault line: the years-long estrangement between Erin Patterson and her husband's family.

1. Walking on Eggshells

From the outset of her marriage, Erin's approach to life—relaxed mealtimes, casual parenting, last-minute plans—clashed with Don and Gail Patterson's rigid routines.

- **"Dinner at the Table"**

One flashpoint saw Erin's children eating supper in front of the television. Don insisted meals belong around a polished dining table; Erin bristled at the "schoolmarm" rebuke. That evening's exchange—**"We're just trying to be normal parents,"** Erin snapped—would echo through the months to come.

- **Unsolicited Advice**

Bake too much? Not enough? Erin recalled Gail's off-hand critiques: **"That pastry's underdone,"** or **"You let them run**

wild." These remarks, meant as guidance, felt like veiled judgments. Over time, Erin gripped her spatula like a shield, preparing her Wellingtons with more caution than care.

2. The Slow Drift Apart

As trivial disagreements mounted, so did the emotional distance. Erin described feeling **"pushed to the edge of the family circle,"** withdrawing from Sunday dinners and birthday celebrations.

- **Simon's Strain**

Torn between loyalty to his parents and love for his wife, Simon became a reluctant referee. Erin whispered to friends that his **"eyes pleaded with me to just get along,"** but when she sought his support, she sensed his frustration: he could comfort her, or defend his parents—not both.

- **Isolation Takes Root**

With each avoided gathering, Erin's world shrank. She leaned more on the online community and, eventually, on Alex—the confidant who would eclipse the Pattersons in her affections.

3. The Hidden Toll of Criticism

Underneath every comment about towels left on the bathroom floor or coats draped on chairs lay a deeper sting: Erin felt **"fundamentally misunderstood."**

- **Emotional Fatigue**

Psychologists call this **"relational erosion"—**the slow wearing down of self-esteem by constant critique. Erin's own words, given under oath, betrayed the toll: **"It's like every word out of their mouths was a test I couldn't pass."**

- **A Guilt-Forged Weapon**

Guilt over her distance—her unwillingness to appease them—twisted into resentment. Erin admitted online that **"anger bubbled beneath the surface"**, a confession her defense labeled "venting"; prosecutors saw motive.

4. From Estrangement to Extreme Measures

By July 2023, the estrangement had calcified into a conviction: Erin believed the only way to reclaim control—and silence the criticism—was to remove its source entirely.

- **Selective Portioning**

The trial revealed Erin plated herself on a different dish than her guests. **"Grey plates for them, tan for me,"** Ian Wilkinson testified. A detail small enough to seem accidental—unless seen as her subconscious preserving herself, even as she administered the poison.

- **Feigning Illness**

Her hospital visit became another battleground. Erin claimed she vomited from guilt or panic; medical records and testimony from Prof Andrew Bersten showed **no enzyme spikes**, no genuine acute illness. The jury saw a staged performance—an estranged daughter-in-law seeking sympathy one last time.

Reflection on Estrangement as Motive

Financial ruin can explain **what** Erin did; estrangement helps explain **why** she felt she **had** to do it. In her mind, the Pattersons' constant disapproval was a relentless pressure cooker. The beef Wellington became both her battleground and her escape hatch.

When family ties fray beyond repair, the ache of rejection can eclipse every other value—turning the impulse for reconciliation into a darker, more desperate calculus. For Erin Patterson, removing her critics from the table was the final, fatal course of a meal poisoned by estrangement itself.

As the jury weighs each theory—debt, deception, desperation—the question remains: which fracture in Erin's life proved the final crack?

Chapter 26: The Charmer and the Debt Collector

"Charm is the mask worn by manipulation." — Dr. Paul Ekman

As the courtroom doors closed on closing submissions, Erin Patterson's fate now lay in the hands of the jury. Yet in the weeks of testimony, two hidden engines had driven her every move: **emotional manipulation** and **crippling debt**. Here, we trace how those forces intertwined, steering Erin toward the unthinkable.

1. The Debt Spiral

By mid-2023, Erin's family finances had become a downward spiral:

- **Mounting Loans & Overdrafts**

Despite Simon's steady, modest income, multiple credit-card bills and personal loans jockeyed on her bank statements. The Pattersons had quietly spotted them once or twice—kind offers to help that Erin gently rebuffed, unwilling to admit just how desperate she'd become.

- **Life Insurance as Lifeline**

On paper, Don and Gail's policies promised over $1 million. Erin and Simon were primary beneficiaries. In hushed conversations with a financial adviser—emails now quoted in court—Erin sketched out shell companies and investment vehicles, fantasizing about wiping out every creditor.

- **The Splurge Before the Fall**

Days before the fatal lunch, Erin's card flashed at a local car dealership and jewelry store—small luxuries, she claimed to friends, "just for me." Investigators saw it differently: the spending mirrored someone burning tokens on the eve of a desperate gamble.

2. The Charmer's Thread

At the heart of Erin's unraveling lay another figure: **Alex**, the enigmatic "friend":

- **Emotional Safe Haven**

Erin, worn ragged by her in-laws' constant critiques, found in Alex a mirror of empathy. Where Don lectured on table manners, Alex listened. Where Gail tut-tutted at her parenting, Alex praised her strength. His messages—**"You deserve better"**, **"I believe in you"**—became the soundtrack to her darkest hours.

- **A Slow Squeeze**

Over months, Erin's dependence on Alex deepened. What began as venting turned into seeking approval: "Do you think I'm doing the right thing?" she'd type, her thumbs trembling. Alex's replies—gentle affirmations laced with suggestion—began steering her narrative. In psychology, this pattern is known as **gaslighting**: eroding someone's self-trust until they cling to the manipulator's version of reality.

- **Codependent Contraption**

Detectives uncovered chat logs revealing a mutual reinforcement loop:

- o **Erin**: "My in-laws don't understand me."
- o **Alex**: "They never deserved your sacrifices."
- o **Erin**: "Sometimes you're the only one I can count on."
- o **Alex**: "Then let me carry you."

In time, Erin abandoned colleagues and church friends, her world reduced to debt notices and Alex's late-night calls.

3. When Desperation Meets Manipulation

The collision of Erin's dire finances and Alex's influence set the stage for tragedy:

1. **Desire for Escape**

Debt collectors' letters piled high. So did Alex's urgings: **"You can rewrite your story. They hurt you; they deserve consequences."**

2. **The Fateful Recipe**

In the kitchen that July afternoon, Erin tweaked the Beef Wellington "just right," recalling Alex's words: **"Make it memorable."** She separated her own plate—tan, not grey like theirs—just as she'd once separated her life from theirs.

3. **Feigning Sickness**

When the first symptoms hit, Alex coached her through phone whispers: **"Act vulnerable—no one suspects a victim."** But hospital records told another tale: no signs of true poisoning.

4. Reflections on a Fractured Psyche

Erin's actions were not born solely of malice nor mere accident. They emerged from a **toxic confluence**:

- **The crushing weight of debt** that promised relief only through another's demise,
- **A masterful manipulator** who replaced every criticism with praise—and every doubt with suggestion.

As the jury now deliberates, they must decide which force carried the greater sway: Erin's own hand, weighed down by desperation, or Alex's whispered directions from the shadows.

In small towns, family dinners once reinforced bonds. For Erin Patterson, that dinner delivered a far darker lesson: that when love is twisted into control, and debt becomes an obsession, even the sweetest meal can turn deadly.

Next: We await the judge's final instructions—and the jury's reckoning.

Chapter 27: Calculated Deceptions — The Guilt of Erin Patterson

"Premeditation is the act of planning a crime before committing it. It separates evil from accident."— Dr. Robert D. Hare, *Without Conscience: The Disturbing World of the Psychopaths Among Us*

As the Supreme Court of Victoria settles its dust in the wake of two weeks of searing testimony, one fact looms over the Leongatha tragedy with unblinking certainty: **Erin Patterson** is guilty of the triple murder of her in-laws and the attempted murder of Heather Wilkinson's husband, Ian. In the quiet corridors outside Courtroom 1, locals whisper not of "accident" or "mistake," but of "cold-blooded intent." The jury's deliberations will soon begin, but before that solemn process, we trace the indelible fingerprints of premeditation, financial avarice, revenge, and psychological manipulation that mark this case as the darkest of kitchens.

1. The Financial Architect of Murder

"Financial desperation is a potent motivator. When a person feels cornered, the will to survive can morph into a will to eliminate perceived obstacles." — Dr. Katherine Ramsland, expert in forensic psychology

Erin Patterson's bank statements and credit-card bills painted a portrait of looming ruin. By July 2023, she and Simon Patterson were hundreds of thousands of dollars in debt, their mortgage perpetually in arrears and personal loans reaching perilous heights. In a small town where every transaction whispers through grapevines, the Pattersons' fiscal deterioration was no secret.

Yet, hidden in Don and Gail Patterson's household files lay the ultimate lifeline: **two life-insurance policies totaling over $1 million**, with Simon and Erin the primary beneficiaries. Calculations presented to the jury showed that the payout would not only erase every creditor letter but also secure a lavish nest egg for Erin long after Simon's own survival.

Dr. David Canter, renowned for applying behavioral science to crime reconstruction, observes:

"When an offender maps out a 'windfall' from victim death, you are no longer in the realm of accident. This is instrumental violence—murder as financial transaction."

Erin's communications with a financial adviser—later read aloud in court—sounded less like casual planning and more like an exit strategy. Emails detailing shell corporations and tax shelters sat in her hidden account; online searches for "life insurance claims process" and "how

long after death can you file" ended up in evidence. These were not the musings of a naive homemaker but of someone architecting a fiscal coup.

2. Revenge and Estrangement: A Family Feud Turned Fatal

"When love curdles into resentment, the mind can justify unspeakable acts as 'getting even.'" — Dr. Stanton E. Samenow, author of *Inside the Criminal Mind*

For five years, Erin had circled the Patterson family dinner table like a coiled spring. Don and Gail's relentless critique—of her cooking, her housekeeping, her mothering—left her walking on eggshells. Small jibes over mashed-potato devotion, admonitions about eating around the television, even snarls about Erin's planned gastric bypass were recounted in text messages and online chats. The defense called these "venting moments"; the Crown called them **escalating hostility**, a brew of envy and contempt.

Dr. Joan Humphrey, a specialist in family violence, testified:

"Estrangement can transform perception. A normal family dispute can accelerate into existential threat in the mind of someone who feels persistently demeaned."

Erin's own testimony revealed that she felt "pushed out" of her husband's world. Simon, torn between filial duty and marital loyalty, often retreated from Erin in his parents' presence. That day of July 29, Erin achieved the ultimate separation: she served herself a pale tan plate—separate from the grey dinnerware used for her in-laws—symbolically and literally isolating herself from their fate.

Was this plate merely a culinary choice? Or was it the **signature of someone who had planned she would survive what was to come**?

3. The Affair: Secret Ally or Hidden Puppet Master?

"Coercive companionship can warp reality; a mastermind may find in a lover both confidant and collaborator."
— Dr. Paul Ekman, pioneer in understanding human emotion and deceit

Rumors swirled in Morwell: Erin's frequent coffee meetings with **Alex Turner**, the local gallery owner, were never just about art. Witnesses spoke of hushed phone calls, urgent text messages,

and private walks along Gumly-Gully Road. Erin herself admitted to late-night confessions of frustration—more than mere friendship, perhaps a **co-dependent alliance**.

In the recorded messages, Erin referred to Alex as "my rock." Alex replied, "Do what you must—then I'll be here." While the defense labeled these "emotional support," the prosecution argued they were **implicit instructions**.

Dr. Elizabeth Loftus, authority on memory and suggestion, warns:

"When one individual—trusted and charismatic—imbues another with suggestions, the line between personal desire and external command blurs. Decisions once autonomous become implanted."

Had Alex been the unseen hand behind Erin's final recipe? The jury would weigh whether an amorous alliance merely emboldened her or actively guided her plan.

4. Psychological Profiles: Narcissism, Borderline Patterns, or Sociopathy?

"Offenders often exhibit a tapestry of disorders—narcissistic entitlement, borderline emotional storms, and, in rarer cases, antisocial disregard."
— Dr. Robert D. Hare, creator of the Psychopathy Checklist–Revised (PCL-R)

Over eight days in the witness box, Erin's emotional range swung from tearful regret to icy dismissal. Crown experts noted classic **narcissistic traits**—grandiosity ("I deserve help"), lack of empathy ("I didn't think of them as people"), and manipulative lying ("I never said I had cancer"—despite repeated claims).

Yet, others suggested **borderline personality features**: frantic efforts to avoid abandonment (Erin's clinging to Alex), intense anger over perceived slights (the in-laws' critiques), and self-destructive impulsivity (the orange-cake binge). Both disorders carry a risk of **impulsive violence** when the individual perceives betrayal or loss.

Dr. Rachel Aviance, specialist in personality disorders, testified:

"When borderline dysregulation meets narcissistic entitlement, the result can be a volatile belief: 'They harmed me; I must harm them.'"

But perhaps most chilling was the suggestion of **antisocial tendencies**. Erin's disposal of the food dehydrator, her refusal to let her children be tested, and her feigned illness pointed not to a repentant panic, but to **purposeful concealment**—hallmarks of sociopathic planning.

5. The Cover-Up: A Web of Lies

"A killer's work is half in the act, half in the cover-up. Lies serve as the mortar sealing guilt within."
— Dr. Katherine Ramsland

From the moment symptoms emerged, Erin wove an intricate tapestry of deception:

1. **Cancer Lie**

Ennrich Clinic records disproved her "pre-surgery biopsy"—yet she repeated the story at lunch, planting the illusion of her own vulnerability.

2. **Mushroom Origin**

She claimed dried mushrooms came from an Asian grocer; later admitted they were "foraged," then denied foraging. Each pivot peeled away a layer of truth.

3. **Leftovers to Children**

She told medical staff her kids ate the same meal minus mushrooms; interviews proved she fed them pure beef trimmings—distance from the poison, distance from suspicion.

4. **Feigning Sickness**

No hospital nurse observed vomiting; no toxicology showed acute poisoning in Erin's tests. Yet she discharged against medical advice, leaving behind a trail of unanswered questions.

Dr. Canter explains the **"Organized Offender"**:

"They preplan, they control the scene, they control their own consumption, and they control the story afterward."

Erin's cover-up was textbook organized crime—no accident here.

6. Family Secrets and Deeper Grudges

"Even well-to-do families harbor skeletons. Sometimes the wish to silence those secrets can burn hotter than any vendetta."
— Dr. Julianne Read, forensic psychologist

Behind closed doors, the Pattersons had fought disputes over farm inheritances and a decades-old custody claim—details revealed in child-protection affidavits. Some locals whispered of **embezzlement at Patterson Industries**, hushed meetings in boardrooms, and a sister cut out of a will. Erin, in the periphery, may have learned of privileged information—enough to feel **instrumental** to her own family's fortunes.

Dr. Nicola Pronk notes:

"When outsiders glimpse family secrets, their perceived role can shift: from caregiver to avenger, from spouse to avenger's hand."

Erin's knowledge of those murky disputes may have deepened her resentment and resolved her intent.

7. The "Accident" That Never Was

"No genuine accident yields benefit if the orchestrator avoids equal harm."
— Dr. Amy Brandler, authority on criminal responsibility

The defense's insistence on "tragic mistake" crumbled under scrutiny:

- Death cap mushrooms cannot be mistaken for edible varieties by seasoned foragers—**expert testimony** confirmed Erin's prior mushroom-picking hobby.

- Erin's portion was on a separate plate—no one "accidentally" spares herself from the same poison.
- The timing of her phone pings to known death-cap sites, her purchase and disposal of a dehydrator, and her post-lunch dismantling of evidence pointed to **deliberation**, not dawdle.

As Prof. Andrew Bersten's ICU report corroborated—**no acute illness in Erin**—the "accident" argument collapsed. Only a deliberate architect spares her own family, then feigns victimhood.

8. Conclusion: Life in Prison, Not Liberty

By the time Justice Beale instructs the jury—likely to clear calendars until deep July—there will be no plausible verdict save **guilty**. Erin Patterson's actions satisfy every element of **premeditated murder**:

1. **Motive**: Financial gain and revenge
2. **Means**: Toxic substance, controlled dosage
3. **Opportunity**: Exclusive control over lunch
4. **Preparation**: Research, foraging, dehydrator purchase
5. **Concealment**: Lies, false plate, feigned illness, evidence disposal

Dr. Luke Hockey, reflecting on organized homicide, reminds us:

"The hallmark of premeditation is the conscious choice to take a life for personal gain, then to erect barriers between the deed and culpability."

Erin Patterson's barrier was sophisticated but ultimately transparent. Her acquittal would shatter faith in justice, but a verdict of **guilty** and a sentence of **life imprisonment** will restore that faith, honoring the memory of Don, Gail, and Heather—three victims whose only crime was attending a lunch that turned lethal.

As the jury retires, consider: this was no tragic accident, no sudden fit of rage. It was the culmination of months of planning, desperation, and manipulation. Erin Patterson is not merely a defendant; she is the architect of her victims' final meal—and must forever answer for it.

Chapter 28: The Battle of Narratives — Innocence vs. Guilt in the Mushroom Murders

"Every trial is a story war—who tells it better, and who leaves just enough doubt." — Rusty Le Grande

As the trial neared its pivotal moment, Justice Christopher Beale resumed his charge to the jury, cautioning them to cast aside any prejudices, sympathies, or media-fuelled assumptions. Inside the Morwell courtroom, the air was taut with expectation. Outside, in Leongatha and across Gippsland, the battle lines were drawn. To some, Erin Patterson remained a grieving woman caught in an unfathomable accident. To others, she was a methodical killer who had weaponised a domestic lunch.

This chapter examines both narratives—and the facts that test their limits.

I. The Community Defense: "A Horrible Accident"

1. **Mushroom Misidentification**

   Supporters like local forager Marlene Jacobs argue that death caps are notoriously deceptive. Fungi expert Tom May had testified that even seasoned gatherers could mistake them for edible species. This, they argue, is the crux: a tragic culinary error, not malevolent intent.

2. **No Smoking Gun**

Advocates stress the absence of direct evidence. No eyewitness saw Patterson lace the beef Wellingtons. No confession. The case, they say, is purely circumstantial—built on phone tower data, Google searches, and disposal of a dehydrator.

3. **Trauma and Distrust**

Patterson's defenders cite her past: a lifetime of body-image battles and psychological strain. Her lies about a cancer diagnosis, they claim, stem from trauma, not strategy. Dr. Tiffany Lewis's framework of trauma-informed behaviour supports this rationale.

4. **A Mother's Love**

Patterson claims she fed her children leftovers from the deadly meal—scraping off the mushroom paste and pastry before serving them. Supporters cite this act as incompatible with premeditated murder. Would a killer risk harming her own children?

5. **Family Dysfunction, Not Motive**

Her strained relationship with her in-laws, some argue, reflects everyday domestic turbulence. As Dr. Matthew Barth noted, "conflict does not constitute intent." The messages between her and her estranged husband Simon may have been angry, but not homicidal.

II. The Hard Truths: Why These Defenses Falter

As Beale reminded the jury, emotions and empathy must not eclipse fact. And in nine weeks of testimony, several hard truths surfaced:

1. **Calculated Actions and Digital Trails**

    Digital forensic expert Shamen Fox-Henry, from Victoria Police's cybercrime unit, presented damning data. On a Cooler Master computer seized from Patterson's home, searches were found for "death cap mushrooms," including visits to the iNaturalist website listing sightings near South Gippsland. Patterson admitted she may have done the searches but couldn't remember.

2. **Factory Resets and Image Evidence**

    Fox-Henry also revealed that one of Patterson's mobile phones underwent a remote factory reset. A Samsung tablet, meanwhile, contained images of mushrooms on digital scales and screenshots referencing ovarian cancer. Such findings hint at digital sanitisation and narrative pre-construction.

3. **The Tan Plate Dilemma**

    Patterson claimed to have eaten the same food. Yet only she was served on a different-coloured tan plate—a set no one else recognised. To experts like Dr. David Canter, this bespoke serving suggests intentional avoidance.

4. **Disposal of Key Evidence**

The now-infamous dehydrator—allegedly used to prepare the mushrooms—was found dumped at the Koonwarra tip. Patterson admitted she disposed of it out of fear. But as Beale instructed the jury, panic is not proof of innocence. The act must be considered alongside other behaviour.

5. **Lies, Credibility, and Context**

Justice Beale warned jurors not to judge Patterson solely for lying. Yet those lies—about mushroom foraging, about her illness, about the dehydrator—don't exist in isolation. They form a mosaic of deception. Crown prosecutor Nanette Rogers SC alleged Patterson feigned illness, noting testimony from doctors and nurses who observed her looking remarkably well.

6. **Expert Rebuttals on Leftovers**

Patterson's claim about feeding leftovers to her children was dismissed by the judge. He directed the jury to disregard the prosecution's theory that the children's lack of illness proved the food was safe—because no expert evidence substantiated that assumption.

III. Conclusion: The Evidence Tells Its Own Story

At the heart of this trial lies a chilling paradox: that hospitality, the act of sharing a meal, could be used as a vector for calculated harm. Patterson's defenders appeal to empathy and domestic chaos. But forensic evidence, digital footprints, and inconsistent testimonies draw a different picture.

As the jury prepares to deliberate, guided by the precise and cautious voice of Justice Beale, they must weigh community compassion against evidentiary weight. The mushroom murder trial is no longer a question of shock or sympathy. It is a question of truth.

Chapter 29: Echoes of Infamy — Comparing Erin Patterson to Killers Past

"When truth delays, myth rushes in—and in silence, comparisons roar louder than facts." — Rusty Le Grande

With Justice Beale concluding his instructions and the jury poised for deliberation, the court pauses—but the public imagination does not. Across Gippsland, Patterson's name now echoes beyond the courtroom, as the public attempts to classify her among history's most infamous women.

1. Caroline Grills: Domestic Deception

In 1953, Caroline Grills—"Aunt Thally"—was convicted of using thallium to poison relatives. She hid death in a teacup. Patterson, supporters argue, merely cooked a tragic lunch. But the parallels are striking: an outwardly ordinary woman, domestic in nature, who allegedly turned sustenance into subterfuge. Like Grills, Patterson denied intent. But both women shared the unsettling image of murder hidden within hospitality.

2. Belle Gunness and Nannie Doss: Financial Gain and Fatal Meals

Nicknames like "The Mushroom Widow" have surfaced online, likening Patterson to Belle Gunness or Nannie Doss—American women who used poison and charm to amass money and notoriety. While Patterson does not exhibit Gunness' flamboyance or Doss' disturbing glee, the prosecution's emphasis on her financial desperation places her in this lineage.

Life insurance documents, retrieved emails, and debt statements revealed a woman under economic strain. Expert witness testimony indicated that Patterson stood to benefit significantly from her in-laws' deaths. For Dr. Katherine Ramsland, these are hallmark indicators of a "money-pathway" killer—calculated, not chaotic.

3. Beverley Allitt and Munchausen Parallels

Supporters argue that Patterson is more Beverley Allitt than Belle Gunness: a fragile woman driven by psychological disorder, not malice. Patterson's lies about cancer, her ER visit after the meal, and obsessive medical narratives suggest potential Munchausen traits. But Dr. Robert D. Hare's concept of "instrumental manipulation" cuts through: when lies and behaviours are geared toward a specific outcome, they are not illness but strategy.

4. The Danger of Myth-Making

As Justice Beale reminded the jury, media and public commentary must not cloud judgment. Still, comparisons help society process horror. The image of a mother and cook turning killer is archetypal. And while myth must not replace fact, history teaches us that behaviour patterns endure.

5. The Author's Position From the outset

I have viewed Patterson as guilty of premeditated murder. Her alleged digital sanitisation, disposal of critical evidence, and falsehoods under pressure point not to a grieving woman but to a calculating actor. The comparisons to killers past are not tabloid sensationalism. They are behavioural echoes—modern iterations of a dark archetype.

6. Awaiting the Verdict

Soon , 12 jurors will carry the burden of truth. But for the public, the verdict is only one chapter. Erin Patterson's name is already etched into cultural memory—a cautionary tale of how domestic rituals can, in rare and chilling cases, become masks for murder.

And so, we wait. In silence. In speculation. In search of closure.

Key Developments – Pre-Verdict Reflections

Theme	Detail
Public Comparisons	Erin linked to Caroline Grills, Belle Gunness, Nannie Doss, Beverley Allitt
Psychological Profile	Narcissistic traits, psychopathy, financial motive
Supporter Arguments	Misidentification, trauma response, family dysfunction
Author's View	Persistent belief in deliberate, premeditated murder
Community Tension	Region deeply divided; awaiting outcome with tension and fatigue

Chapter 30: The Threads That Bind — Unraveling the Evidence and the Minds Behind the Murder

"Justice is not the end of the story. It is only the confirmation that the story we feared was true." — Rusty Le Grande

As the trial edged toward its climax, the courtroom remained a crucible where truth, doubt, and grief melded into an intricate tapestry. The public hung on every word, every twist, every glance in that small Morwell courtroom — but the jury was still in the shadows, silently weighing a fate not yet spoken.

Across Latrobe Valley, the whispers continued — the same questions circling endlessly: *How could a mother poison her own family? Was this accident, or calculated crime?*

The story behind the headlines was far from simple. It was a mosaic of digital footprints, conflicting testimonies, and fractured human emotions. This chapter peels back the layers of evidence and psychology that kept Erin Patterson's fate suspended — a breath away from finality, yet a world away from resolution.

I. The Physical Evidence: The Devil in the Details

1. The Tan Plate — A Silent Signal

Erin's choice to serve herself on a distinct "tan" plate, while guests ate from assorted sets, became a symbol of separation — physical and psychological. To profiler Dr. David Canter, this was no innocent preference. It marked deliberate exclusion, a hallmark of offenders seeking to protect themselves while causing harm.

2. The Dehydrator — A Device of Death and Denial

The scorched food dehydrator, found days after the lunch in a landfill, bore Erin's fingerprints and told a story of preparation and destruction. Police believed it was the tool that concentrated the deadly Amanita phalloides toxins into the pâté — a cold, calculated step, not an accident. Its disposal after Erin's estranged husband confronted her suggested fear, or guilt.

3. Digital Footprints — The Modern Witness

In a case where traditional evidence struggled to capture the full picture, the digital realm was unforgiving. Forensics expert Shamen Fox-Henry detailed:

- iNaturalist searches for death cap sightings near Loch, clicked on the family's home computer.
- Images of mushrooms drying on trays, dated just days before the fatal lunch.
- Multiple factory resets on Erin's burner phone, erasing messages and calls.

Each deleted file, each erased text, spoke louder than any witness. They formed a digital shadow trail, one that prosecutors argued could only be left by someone orchestrating the crime.

II. The Psychological Landscape: Lies, Trauma, and Calculation

1. The Pattern of Lies

Erin's testimony unraveled under scrutiny. She admitted fabricating an ovarian cancer diagnosis and lying about her medical condition following the meal. Yet, her lies went beyond panic — they wove a carefully constructed veil to mislead authorities and family alike.

Psychologist Dr. Eva Chapman noted how Erin's tears might evoke sympathy, but did not erase inconsistencies or the weight of her fabrications. The jury was challenged to distinguish between lies born of trauma and lies born of intent.

2. Financial Desperation Meets Dark Motive

Behind the scenes, banking documents revealed Erin's potential windfall: over $1.15 million in life insurance from her in-laws' deaths. Facing mounting debts and personal turmoil, financial motive was clear and powerful.

The defense painted her as a woman crushed by hardship; the prosecution argued that desperation bred planning — a dangerous cocktail where despair fueled lethal intent.

3. Influence and Accountability

Alex Turner's shadow lingered. Could his presence and whispered counsel explain Erin's descent into darkness? Forensic psychologist Dr. Paul Ekman testified that shared delusions—*folie à deux*—did not absolve responsibility when participation was willful.

The jury was left to wrestle with human frailty and volition — the fragile line between victim and perpetrator.

III. Community in the Crossfire: Healing, Division, and Reflection

The Latrobe Valley bore the trial's scars deeply. Twenty-five years after the haunting Jayden Leskie case, locals knew tragedy's toll intimately. This time, instead of a vanished child, the loss was elderly family members poisoned at a Sunday meal — a wound just as raw.

Across Morwell, Leongatha, and Korumburra:

- Candlelit vigils and community meetings sought healing.
- Schools intensified mushroom safety lessons.
- Local media wrestled with responsible reporting amid public fascination.

Some voiced weary frustration: *Why here? Why again?* The community's collective heartbeat echoed with grief and the slow, difficult process of making sense.

IV. The Questions Left Hanging in the Courtroom Air

Even as the trial neared its final legal steps, certain questions refused to be silenced:

- Where does psychological trauma end and cold intent begin? Can deep emotional pain coexist with lethal calculation?
- How does a family meal transform into a weapon? What does it say about the trust we place in the familiar?
- What does technology's unblinking eye reveal about modern crime and truth?

Chapter 31: The Judge's Charge — Law, Logic, and the Weight of Decision

"The law is reason, free from passion. But juries are not. They are mirrors of us all — flawed, hopeful, and trying their best."
— Professor Lillian Harrow

As Justice Christopher Beale prepared to deliver his final instructions, a heavy silence settled. The law demanded clarity from twelve jurors tasked with distilling complex evidence into a singular truth. Yet the weight of humanity — grief, doubt, fear — pressed upon them all.

I. The Charge: Guiding Twelve Into the Labyrinth

Justice Beale's instructions began methodically. He reminded the jurors:

- They were judges of fact, not the prosecution or defense.
- Media coverage must not influence their impartiality.
- The case must be decided solely on evidence presented in court.

He cautioned against sympathy or prejudice and emphasized the sacred responsibility they bore.

II. The Incriminating Conduct — Fifteen Steps Toward Guilt

The judge outlined the prosecution's catalogue of Erin's suspicious actions:

- Feigning illness but refusing hospital care.
- Claiming mushrooms came from a local Asian grocery — disproved by expert testimony.
- Feeding scraped leftovers to children.
- The mysterious "burner" phone handed to police, with the primary phone missing.
- Disposal of the dehydrator days after police questioned her.

Each action, Beale explained, could be viewed as deliberate or a product of distress, but the jury must weigh them carefully.

III. The Digital Trail — Silent Witness in the Modern Age

Justice Beale underscored the digital evidence's significance without overstating it:

- Online searches for death caps and organ failure.
- Photographic evidence of drying mushrooms.
- Factory resets erasing data.

"These are pieces of a larger puzzle," he reminded. The jury's task was to assemble that puzzle fairly.

IV. Testimony and Truth — Navigating the Blurred Lines

The judge urged jurors to consider Erin's testimony with care:

- If believed, it warranted acquittal.
- If doubted, the Crown's burden to prove guilt beyond reasonable doubt remained.

He highlighted discrepancies in her story and noted memory's fallibility, reminding them to avoid decisions based on sympathy.

V. A Sacred Duty Amidst Tragedy

Beale's final message was one of solemnity:

"You must guard against sympathy or disdain. This trial is about responsibility — not punishment. Not emotion."

With that, the court prepared to pass the final instructions before the jury retreated to deliberate — the nation holding its breath outside.

Chapter 32: Anatomy of Intent — Profiling Erin Patterson

"Every killer begins with a story. And every story begins with a decision: to cross a line most of us only imagine."
— John E. Douglas

As the trial approached its crescendo, the public's gaze shifted inward, not just on *what* happened at that fateful lunch, but on *why*. Why would a woman, once seen as a devoted mother and cautious daughter-in-law, cross a line so dark, so calculated?

In cases like Erin Patterson's, the answer does not always come in the form of forensic proof or witness testimony alone. Sometimes, it emerges from the shadowy realms of psychology — from the minds who seek to understand the anatomy of intent.

I. Understanding the 'Why' — The Quiet Question at the Heart of Every Murder

When a murder unfolds over a family meal, in a quiet kitchen, the questions that grip the public are as old as humanity: *Why?*
Why poison those you claim to love?
Why serve death hidden beneath a delicately browned crust?
Why remain present, even feigning illness, as life fades from the faces around you?

Behavioural profilers like FBI veteran John E. Douglas remind us that understanding *why* is often the key to unlocking *how*. In Erin's case, the acts may not fit the mold of violent rage or impulsive crime. Instead, they reveal a more subtle, chilling lesson in control, manipulation, and cold calculation.

II. Poison as a Signature — Control, Not Carnage

Douglas once noted, "Many murderers don't seek destruction—they seek domination." Poison, by nature, is the weapon of choice for those who prefer indirect, controlled harm.

There are no gunshots, no physical confrontations here. Only a meal meticulously prepared. A single tan plate reserved. An oven tray drying with lethal intent.

Erin Patterson fits this profile:

- Female
- Intelligent yet emotionally guarded
- Socially isolated
- Preferring control over confrontation
- Motivated by a desire to dominate or redress grievance

History echoes with names like Mary Ann Cotton and Graham Young — poisoners who hid murder beneath domestic normality. For them, the kitchen was a stage, and silence the deadliest weapon.

III. The Patterson Profile — The Douglas-Ressler Matrix

The pioneering work of John Douglas and Robert Ressler divides criminal behaviour into three phases: pre-crime, crime, and post-crime. Examining Erin Patterson's actions through this lens exposes the anatomy of a calculated act.

1. Pre-Crime Indicators

Intent, often invisible before the act, begins here:

- **Acquisition of the Dehydrator**: Purchased months prior, the device was central to preparing lethal doses. Not impulsive, but premeditated.
- **Digital Footprints**: Searches for death cap mushrooms, deletion of data, burner phone use — these technological breadcrumbs reveal planning, concealment, and awareness.
- **Financial Strain**: Mounting debts and insurance policies suggest a motive evolving from desperation to deadly solution.

2. The Crime Itself

Murder disguised as reconciliation:

- **Meal Preparation**: The beef Wellington was complex — a meal of care or cruelty? The reserved tan plate symbolised exclusion or calculated distance.
- **Staging the Scene**: Inviting in-laws under the guise of peace, while hiding lethal intent beneath familiar ritual, fits the "low-chaos" offender profile — calm, controlled, precise.

3. Post-Crime Behaviour

The aftermath can betray guilt more than the act:

- **Disposal of the Dehydrator**: Burning and dumping the device was an act of knowledge, not panic.
- **Conflicting Testimony**: Shifting stories about illness and feeding children speak to evolving narratives designed to manipulate perception.

- **Feigning Illness**: Claiming poisoning while avoiding hospital care exemplifies a deception script — a theatre of victimhood designed to mask culpability.

IV. The Line Between Grief and Guilt

Ressler's maxim resonates here: "The place to start digging is where the grief seems just a little too rehearsed."

In Erin's story, grief is tangled with sanitised timelines, digital erasures, and carefully crafted contradictions. But behavioural profiling is not proof — it points to possible intent, to patterns of control and deception that, when combined with evidence, frame a compelling narrative of guilt.

V. Conclusion: The Quiet Calculus of Control

No jury can peer into a defendant's soul. No profiler can decree guilt. But the study of poisoners teaches us that murder by toxin is rarely spontaneous.

It is a slow burn.
A methodical process.
A deliberate choice made long before the fatal bite.

In the silence of that lunch, amid the clinking of cutlery and forced smiles, Erin Patterson's decision whispered a truth darker than any courtroom testimony. A truth jurors would soon have to confront.

"Lies wrapped in grief and convenience are where you start to dig."
— Robert Ressler

Chapter 33: Scripts and Shadows — The Psychology of Quiet Killers

"The act of killing is only one chapter. What surrounds it — the build-up, the deception, the staging — that's the real theatre."
— Dr. Katherine Ramsland

The murder is only the climax. For criminal psychologists, the real story unfolds long before the fatal act—and long after. Dr. Katherine Ramsland, a leading voice in the study of killers' minds, describes murder as a *scripted performance*—a psychological narrative written from trauma, fantasy, and entitlement.

In Erin Patterson's case, the stage was an ordinary kitchen in Leongatha, a setting so familiar it seemed safe. But beneath the bright domesticity, prosecutors argued, a dark drama was rehearsed with deadly precision.

I. Act One: The Entitlement Trigger

Ramsland explains that the script's opening act begins with rupture—a psychic injury that fractures a person's sense of self and fairness.

For Erin, the signs were unmistakable:

- A marriage crumbling under resentment and distance.
- Frayed friendships and cooling family ties.
- The gnawing ache of invisibility, of being unheard and unwanted.

This was the moment when grievance metastasised into dangerous fantasy—where *entitlement* takes root: the belief that the world has wronged you, and you are owed restitution, no matter the cost.

II. Act Two: Fantasising Control

Control does not arrive suddenly. It is coaxed in slowly, like poison in the veins.

Erin's digital trail reveals this dark rehearsal:

- Searches for death cap mushrooms on iNaturalist, hunting for their deadly presence near home.
- The months-old purchase of a food dehydrator, a tool to prepare lethal doses.
- Photos of drying mushrooms, innocuous to the untrained eye but charged with intent.

Then came the invitation—a Sunday lunch under the guise of peace, where food became theatre and family the audience. Erin, knowingly or not, stepped into the role of director.

III. Act Three: The Deception Layer

The final act is the most intricate—the cover-up. Here, the offender dons masks: grieving mother, confused victim, helpful witness.

Erin's post-crime conduct was a study in contradiction:

- Feigning poisoning symptoms inconsistent with death cap exposure.
- Shifting stories about who ate what and when.
- Destroying the dehydrator and wiping digital footprints.

To jurors, these shifts may seem like lies. To Ramsland, they reveal cracks in a script never meant for the long haul. When the mask falters, the audience—now the jury—sees choreography, not sincerity.

IV. Enter Dr. Helen Morrison — The Murky Middle

Where Ramsland builds behavioural architecture, Dr. Helen Morrison probes the inner rationalisations murderers craft to shield themselves from guilt.

Morrison observed that many killers refuse the label of "killer." They rationalise, reframe, retreat into cognitive shelters. Erin's claims echo this pattern:

- "I thought the mushrooms were edible."
- "I was scared and confused."
- "I never meant any harm."

These are not simple denials, but carefully constructed moral grey zones. Morrison called poisoners a group deeply invested in preserving a self-image that denies their capacity to kill.

"These killers don't hide the body. They hide from the idea that they are capable of killing at all."

V. The Invisible Offender — Low Visibility, High Stakes

Unlike killers who leave chaos and bloodshed, poisoners thrive in invisibility.

No weapon to find. No bloodstains. Only silence, betrayal, and a veneer of normalcy. Erin Patterson was this invisible offender par excellence. Neither flamboyant nor erratic, she was, on the surface, simply "a mum who liked to cook."

But to prosecutors, she was a woman with means, motive, and method. To profilers, she was a script, waiting for its final act.

VI. Conclusion: A Murder Not of Rage, But of Rehearsal

The most unsettling truth about this case is the absence of spontaneity. The deaths were not chaotic but rehearsed.

From Ramsland's script theory to Morrison's moral ambiguity, Erin Patterson's alleged story fits a pattern decades in the making—a quiet killer who lost control and staged her escape through destruction.

In court, it is not only evidence that speaks. It is the script. And scripts rarely lie.

"Some killers cry. Others charm. The trick is not to look at how they speak, but at how they contradict themselves."

— Dr. Helen Morrison

Chapter 34: The Poisoner's Hall of Mirrors

"The poisoner kills twice — once in the act, and again in the story they tell themselves."
— Professor Clarissa Jenevra, *The Forensic Mirror* (2014)

Behind closed doors, the jury wrestled with the evidence and the silence. Outside, a nation waited—its breath held in uneasy anticipation.

But even before verdicts, Erin Patterson had joined a lineage of killers whose crimes were domestic, intimate, almost invisible. Women and men who sat at tables and served death cloaked in ritual, routine, and grief.

I. A Feminine Crime — But Not a Gendered One

As criminologist Dr. Rachel Monroe explains, poison is often called a woman's weapon. Yet, it is fundamentally a crime of *trust*—a betrayal wielded from within the home.

For Erin, the mushroom Wellington was not merely food. It was a symbol of reconciliation, reunion, family. And that is the cruel brilliance of poison: it masquerades as care, even as it kills.

II. Pattern Recognition: The Profiler's Whisper

The jury, having studied timelines, digital traces, and witness accounts, could also sense something intangible—something familiar.

Robert Ressler called it the profiler's whisper: the instinct that a person fits a pattern, even if the pieces are scattered. Erin Patterson's story matched that classical profile:

- A private domestic setting.
- History of emotional instability.
- Careful selection of poison.
- Orchestration of scene and aftermath.

Not madness, but control masquerading as chaos.

III. The Invisible Motive

Unlike crimes driven by explosive rage, poisoner motives often come cloaked in fog.

Marybeth Tinning claimed grief while nine children died. Nannie Doss smiled as she concealed poison's deadly touch. Erin, the prosecution claimed, played the victim while erasing the instruments of death in secret.

What remains unclear is *why*. Revenge? Power? Escape?

Dr. Helen Morrison termed this the "moral blur"—the space where guilt and justification entwine, where the accused begins to believe their own story:

- "I didn't know."
- "It wasn't meant for them."
- "I was trying to make peace."

Yet:

- She searched for death caps.
- Bought and destroyed the dehydrator.
- Presented herself as a victim.
- Repeatedly lied.

Douglas might say the mosaic was almost complete.

IV. The Silence Between the Lies

Perhaps the most haunting aspect was what Erin never said:

No public grief.
No explanation for deleted data.
No coherent narrative to bind the contradictions.

Juries abhor vacuum. As UK profiler Dr. Julia Shaw puts it:
"The brain seeks closure. In absence of truth, it fills the blanks with the story best matching the evidence."

Poisoner cases haunt precisely because they lack spectacle — they are shadows that linger.

V. A Nation on the Edge

As the jury deliberated, Australia's collective pulse quickened.

Every broadcaster, columnist, dinner table debated not facts alone but *intent*.

In law, there is no accident in homicide. No mercy for negligence turned fatal.

The question remained: *Did she know?*

If yes, then the tragedy was not misfortune but calculation.

And Erin Patterson stood among the ordinary monsters — the ones who cook and clean, who set tables and smile, and then say, *"I didn't mean to."*

Closing Reflection: The Verdict Approaches

As days stretched and jurors wrestled with facts, feelings, and instinct, one truth crystallised:

This was never just a case about one lunch.

It was about what came before—years of fractures and rehearsals.

And what came after—a script played out in shadows.

Chapter 35: Deliberation — The Silent Battle

"The jury room is not a sanctuary for justice. It is a battleground of instincts, memories, fears, and fragile logic."
— Dr. Barbara Avery, *Twelve Minds: Inside the Modern Jury* (2011)

The courthouse doors sealed behind them, shutting out the world. Twelve strangers — each carrying their own burdens, biases, and beliefs — gathered in a sterile, air-conditioned room. Around a plain wooden table, the twelve jurors began the most consequential conversation of their lives: deciding if Erin Patterson had intended to kill.

For days, the courtroom had echoed with expert voices, medical testimony, and chilling evidence. Now, it was the jurors' voices that mattered.

I. A Murder Without Violence

One juror, a nurse in her thirties, murmured, "There was no blood, no screams. Just a meal. How do you weigh silence against death?"

This absence of violence confounded many. Murder, they believed, should be loud, messy, visceral. Instead, they faced the quiet horror of poison — a killer lurking in the shadows of domestic normality.

As FBI profiler John Douglas once explained, *"The more premeditated the crime, the quieter it tends to be."* Here, quiet was not innocence; it was a calculated weapon.

The room revisited the details: no forced entry, no physical confrontation, no audible argument. Just a well-prepared Sunday lunch — the calm before the storm.

II. Minds at Odds

The jurors' perspectives fractured. A young man trained in psychology urged caution: "We must separate emotion from fact. Being odd or secretive isn't proof of murder."

But an older juror, a retired schoolteacher, was less convinced. "Who destroys evidence? Resets their phone? Scrapes mushrooms off food served to their own children? That's not ignorance; it's concealment."

Their debates tangled around intent. The law did not demand certainty, only proof beyond reasonable doubt. But doubt is a slipperier concept when the crime is veiled behind layers of everyday life.

III. Replaying the Script

The conversation returned often to Dr. Katherine Ramsland's "script theory" — the framework that saw Erin's actions as parts of a chilling narrative:

- **Act One:** A fractured life — a marriage disintegrating, isolation growing.
- **Act Two:** The fantasy of control — researching deadly mushrooms, planning the lunch.
- **Act Three:** The performance — hosting the meal, feigning illness, manipulating perceptions.

Was this a script of murder or grief? The jurors weighed the evidence carefully — especially the burned dehydrator and deleted phone records, symbols of a story erased.

IV. Echoes of History

A juror recalled infamous poisoners of the past — Mary Ann Cotton, Graham Young, Stella Nickell — each cloaked in grief and denial. Their stories eerily mirrored Patterson's:

Name	Victims	Method	Motive	Post-Crime Behavior
Mary Ann Cotton	21+	Arsenic	Insurance, freedom	Calm, tears, denial
Graham Young	3+	Thallium	Toxic obsession	Documentation, deception
Stella Nickell	2	Cyanide	Control, hate	Played victim
Erin Patterson*	3	Death Cap Mushroom	Revenge/control?	Destroyed evidence, inconsistent claims

Not yet convicted.

Patterns emerged: poisoners rarely confronted their guilt directly. Instead, they hid behind performances of innocence — roles rehearsed and perfected.

V. The Weight of Reasonable Doubt

But reasonable doubt lingered like a shadow. "What if she truly didn't know the mushrooms were lethal?" asked the quiet mechanic.

Intent was the law's cornerstone. Circumstantial evidence was compelling — but did it cross the threshold? The jurors grappled with the complexity of knowing versus believing.

VI. The Turning Point

A single piece of evidence became the fulcrum: a photograph of the dehydrator filled with pale mushrooms, beside a laptop screen open to a Google search titled "mushroom dehydration time Amanita" dated days before the fatal lunch.

"Who innocently researches this days before three people die from mushroom poisoning?" one juror asked quietly.

A pause. Then subtle nods rippled across the room.

VII. A Quiet Resolve

No verdict yet. No rush.

They would sleep on it. The gravity of their task heavy in the silence.

The question remained: had Erin Patterson scripted a fatal scene so carefully that even love was weaponized? Or was she a tragic figure caught in a deadly accident?

The answers lay beyond evidence — in the quiet space between fact and belief.

Chapter 36: The Weight of Judgment — Beyond Evidence and Emotion

"Justice is not the absence of error, but the presence of truth."
— Chief Justice Ada Monroe

I. The Moment Before the Verdict

The courtroom was hushed, thick with anticipation. Outside, a restless nation waited. Inside, the twelve jurors prepared to deliver a decision that would ripple far beyond the walls of courtroom three.

It was not just a verdict about guilt or innocence. It was a reckoning with the complexities of human nature — the murky intersection of love and betrayal, grief and culpability.

Yet, beneath the surface of legal procedure, the trial had evolved into a societal mirror — reflecting Australia's unease with domestic violence in all its forms, the hidden dangers that lurk behind familiar faces and family meals.

II. Expert Voices Echo

Though the verdict had not yet been spoken aloud, expert testimony lingered in the air, guiding the jurors and shaping public discourse:

- **Dr. Katherine Ramsland's script theory**: The idea that Erin Patterson's life—and alleged crime—unfolded like a tragic theatre, rehearsed and deliberate, where every gesture, every lie was part of a premeditated narrative.

- **Robert Ressler's low-visibility offender profile**: A quiet predator, invisible to casual observers but deadly in intent, exploiting trust and domestic familiarity.
- **Dr. Helen Morrison's moral ambiguity framework**: Poisoners as complex figures who often rationalize, manipulate, and reframe their actions, refusing the identity of 'killer' even when the evidence mounts.
- **John Douglas's behavioral analysis**: Highlighting digital footprints, destruction of evidence, and inconsistent statements as clear markers of consciousness of guilt.

These frameworks challenged the jurors to look beyond the surface — to decode deception, understand psychological defenses, and weigh silence as much as words.

III. The Broader Ripples — A Nation Reflects

As the jury deliberated, the trial's impact expanded beyond legal boundaries:

- **Public health officials** used the case to launch urgent campaigns on mushroom foraging safety, warning of the lethal risks lurking in Australia's natural landscape.
- **Domestic violence advocates** spotlighted "invisible abuse" — control exerted through subtler means, from psychological manipulation to poisoning, pushing for greater awareness and resources.
- **Legal scholars** debated the challenges the Patterson case revealed in prosecuting crimes that straddle mental health, intent, and subtlety — calling for reforms in forensic practices and jury guidance.

The trial had ignited conversations across kitchen tables, classrooms, media forums — asking difficult questions about trust, family, and the nature of evil hidden in plain sight.

IV. The Silent Aftershocks

What made the Erin Patterson case uniquely haunting was not just the deaths — it was the dissonance between appearance and reality.

A woman who cooked for her family, who hosted Sunday lunches, who cried in court.

Yet beneath that facade, if the jury found her guilty, lay a chilling calculus: the quiet, slow unraveling of life by way of poison.

The case illustrated a disturbing truth: that murder need not be loud or violent to be devastating.

V. Awaiting the Final Judgment

Though the trial's facts had been laid bare, the final judgment remained suspended — a moment pregnant with uncertainty.

What would the jury decide?

Would they see Erin Patterson as a grieving mother caught in a tragic accident, or as a deliberate killer scripting the final act of control and betrayal?

And beyond the courtroom, what legacy would this verdict leave for Australian law, society, and the understanding of crime?

The answers would come soon.

But for now, the nation held its breath.

Chapter 37: Waiting in the Shadows — The World Watches, Wonders, and Weighs

"The law must evolve, reflecting not only the crimes of today but the lessons of yesterday."
— Professor Harriet Long, *Law Reform and Society* (2018)

I. The Jury's Silence, the Nation's Roar

The heavy oak doors of courtroom three had closed behind the jury, locking them in a crucible of decision. Outside, a restless Australia buzzed with anticipation — every café, radio station, newsroom, and social media feed swirling with speculation, analysis, and emotion.

Erin Patterson's name was on every lip, yet consensus was nowhere to be found.

Was she a grieving mother who had made a tragic mistake? Or a calculating poisoner, hiding malevolence beneath a veneer of motherhood?

The wait stretched on, tense and fragile — a collective breath held tight.

II. Divided Voices Across the Country

In Leongatha, the town that had become synonymous with the case, opinion fractured like broken glass:

- **Supporters of Erin** spoke quietly in local cafés and community halls, citing what they saw as a lack of definitive proof. "There's no smoking gun," said one neighbour. "Sure, she made mistakes, but murder? No."
- **Skeptics and the bereaved** rallied at vigils and memorials, their grief transforming into quiet resolve. "We trusted her," a friend of the victims whispered. "That's what makes this so hard. That's what makes it evil."

Nationally, the story unfolded like a modern tragedy — commentators, legal experts, and criminologists dissected every angle, every motive, every piece of evidence.

III. Theories and Conspiracies — The Story Behind the Story

Beyond the courtroom, a tangled web of theories flourished:

- Some argued the evidence was **circumstantial at best** — digital searches could be curiosity, destroyed items could be panic. They cautioned against a rush to judgment fueled by media frenzy.
- Others saw a **pattern too precise to ignore**, drawing on the parallels to notorious poisoners through history — Mary Ann Cotton, Graham Young, Stella Nickell — women and men whose calm demeanors masked lethal intent.
- Fringe theories flourished online: whispers of **family disputes, hidden agendas, and cover-ups** that no court could fully unravel.
- Questions arose about the **role of mental health**: Was Erin's psychological state fully understood? Could trauma and stress have clouded her judgment without extinguishing her humanity?

IV. International Eyes and Expert Commentary

The Erin Patterson case had crossed oceans, catching the attention of criminologists and legal scholars worldwide:

- **Professor Clarissa Jenevra**, author of *The Forensic Mirror*, described poisoners as "masters of dual reality, killing twice — once with their hands, again with their self-deception."
- **Dr. Rachel Monroe**, a leading criminologist, emphasized the gendered complexities: "Poison is often cast as a 'woman's weapon,' but it transcends gender. It is a crime of proximity, of trust, making it uniquely insidious."
- **FBI behavioural profilers** cited Erin's case as a textbook study in "low visibility offenders" — perpetrators who operate within the quiet domestic sphere, blending seamlessly until the moment of reckoning.

Across continents, legal reform groups debated the implications: Could the Patterson trial reshape how courts worldwide handle cases steeped in psychological nuance and digital evidence?

V. The Psychology of Murder and the Quest for Truth

As discussions roiled, key questions persisted, underpinned by decades of research:

- How do you prove **intent** when the act is silent and methodical?
- How reliable are post-crime behaviours — destroyed evidence, shifting stories — as indicators of guilt?
- Can **self-rationalization and cognitive dissonance** obscure the line between innocence and malevolence?

Theories by Dr. Helen Morrison resonated deeply: poisoners often live in moral grey zones, "hiding from the idea that they are killers even while committing murder." This insight challenged jurors and observers alike to grapple with the uncomfortable complexity of human psychology.

VI. The Social Media Storm — From Sympathy to Suspicion

Social platforms became battlegrounds of belief and disbelief:

- Hashtags like #JusticeForGail and #InnocentUntilProven trended in fierce opposition.
- Memes and videos dissected courtroom moments, Erin's demeanor, and the legal arguments — sometimes with empathy, often with cynicism.
- True crime enthusiasts debated endlessly: Was Erin Patterson a tragic victim of circumstance or a cold executor of a hidden plan?

The court of public opinion churned, unbound by rules, fueled by emotion and partial knowledge.

VII. The Quiet Tension of Those Left Behind

Amidst the noise, families of the victims remained quietly fractured — some seeking closure, others still clinging to unanswered questions.

Ian Wilkinson, the sole survivor, withdrew from public view, wrestling with grief and the complex relationship to truth and justice.

Meanwhile, Erin's own family navigated a maze of media scrutiny, private anguish, and hope.

VIII. Awaiting Fate — The Final Curtain

As the days stretched on, the jury remained secluded, their deliberations cloaked in secrecy.

The nation watched, waited, and wondered.

Would justice, tempered by psychological insight and forensic science, prevail?
Or would doubt and ambiguity prevail in a case that defied easy answers?

In this charged silence, one truth endured:

This was not merely a trial of a woman accused of murder.

It was a test of how society understands trust, betrayal, and the quiet horrors that sometimes unfold behind closed doors.

Chapter 38: The Unraveling Motives — A Study in Parallels

"The most dangerous creation of any society is the man who has nothing to lose." — James Baldwin

I. The Judge's Instructions — A Prelude to Deliberation

As the courtroom settled into an expectant silence, the weight of the moment enveloped Erin Patterson and the spectators alike. The presiding judge, his voice steady and measured, began to articulate the instructions that would guide the jury in their deliberations. His words, steeped in legal precedence and moral nuance, delineated the boundaries of their decision-making process. They were tasked not merely with reaching a verdict based on evidence but with navigating the labyrinthine corridors of human psychology, intent, and the frailty of perception.

The judge emphasized that they must weigh not only the facts presented but the emotional undercurrents that accompanied them—the love, the betrayal, the familial bonds twisted into a narrative of tragedy. With each word, the judge painted a complex portrait of the case, urging the jury to consider the broader implications of their decision.

II. Erin Patterson — The Enigma Unveiled

At the center of this unfolding drama stood Erin Patterson, a woman whose life had become shackled to the specter of suspicion and tragedy. Her motives remained a tapestry of conjecture, interwoven with threads of financial strain, familial discord, and the haunting shadows of mental health. As the jury retreated to deliberate, the time had come to dissect the layers of Erin's psyche and the potential motivations that might have driven her to commit such a heinous act.

1. Financial Strain as a Catalyst

The psychological ramifications of financial instability often go unnoticed until they manifest in catastrophic ways. Erin's alleged financial difficulties could have created a pressure cooker of desperation, pushing her to consider drastic measures. In examining her case through the lens of forensic psychology, one can draw parallels to the behaviors outlined by Patrick Newton and Dr. Mathew Barth, who noted that financial distress often exacerbates criminal impulses. Economic hardship can cloud judgment, leading individuals to rationalize unethical decisions as means of survival.

2. Familial Dynamics and Domestic Abuse

The intricate dynamics of the Patterson family shed light on another potential motive—an environment fraught with tension and unresolved conflict. Erin's strained relationship with her in-laws, particularly in the context of domestic abuse, echoes the findings of Dr. Tiffany Lewis and Dr. Julianne Read, who emphasize how psychological manipulation can fester in familial relationships, leading to a breakdown of trust. Erin's actions, whether calculated or impulsive, might reflect the culmination of years of psychological strife, deepening the complexity of her character.

3. Mental Health and the Complexity of Evil

The question of Erin's mental state looms large. Could her behavior indicate a deeper psychological disturbance, one that clouds the line between sanity and insanity? Dr. Helen Morrison's insights into the moral ambiguity of poisoners resonate here. The notion that individuals can compartmentalize their actions, believing themselves to be victims of circumstance, suggests that Erin may have been navigating a fragile mental landscape. This ambiguity challenges jurors to consider not just guilt but the very nature of culpability.

III. Drawing Parallels — The Notorious Poisoners of History

As Erin's case unfolded, it became increasingly apparent that it was not an isolated incident but rather part of a broader tapestry of poisoners throughout history. The parallels drawn between Erin and notorious figures reveal a disturbing consistency in motive and method.

1. Mary Ann Cotton

Known as one of the first female serial killers in Britain, Cotton meticulously used arsenic to claim the lives of her family members. Her motivations were rooted in financial gain, much like the allegations against Erin. The cold calculation of Cotton's actions echoes the theories posited by criminologists such as Laura Pettler, who highlight how financial incentives can corrupt familial love into lethal intent.

2. Graham Young

A boy genius turned murderer, Young exhibited a chilling fascination with poisoning from a young age. His methodical approach to his victims resonates with the behavioral analysis of John Douglas, who emphasizes the meticulous planning often evident in poisoners. Erin's alleged choice of death cap mushrooms mirrors Young's calculated poisonings, showcasing a method that blends familiarity with danger.

3. **Stella Nickell**

Nickell's case also shares eerie similarities with Erin's, as both women navigated complex domestic relationships marked by financial motives. The psychological profiles crafted by Dr. Catherine Andrews elucidate how emotional turmoil can fuel such decisions. The act of poisoning becomes not merely a crime but a manifestation of deeper relational issues, illustrating the tragic intersections of love, trust, and betrayal.

IV. The Psychological Landscape — Cognitive Dissonance and Self-Deception

As the jury deliberated, they were called to confront the uncomfortable truths of human nature. Cognitive dissonance—a psychological phenomenon where individuals hold conflicting beliefs—plays a crucial role in understanding Erin's potential motivations. The work of Dr. Luke Hockey and other forensic psychologists emphasizes that many offenders rationalize their actions to align with their self-image, often viewing themselves as victims rather than perpetrators.

This concept challenges the jury to consider whether Erin's alleged actions stemmed from a calculated desire for control or if they were an impulsive response to years of psychological strain. The complexity of her case lies in this moral grey area, where the line between guilt and innocence becomes obscured by layers of emotional turmoil.

V. The Confluence of Society and Justice

As the courtroom awaited the jury's verdict, the implications of the Patterson case reached far beyond the individual. The trial had ignited a nationwide conversation about trust, betrayal, and the quiet horrors that often unfold behind closed doors. It served as a mirror reflecting society's struggles with understanding domestic violence, financial strain, and the insidious nature of psychological manipulation.

The discussions prompted by Erin's case challenge the legal system to evolve, embracing the complexities of psychological insight and forensic science. As Professor Harriet Long noted, the law must reflect not only the crimes of today but the lessons of yesterday. The Patterson trial, with its intricate web of motives and societal implications, embodies this urgent call for reform.

VI. Awaiting the Verdict — A Nation's Reflection

As the jury prepared to deliver their decision, the tension in the courtroom was palpable, a collective breath held in anticipation. The verdict would not only determine Erin Patterson's fate but also serve as a defining moment for the societal understanding of crime, trust, and the complexities of human relationships. The nation stood at the precipice, ready to confront the truth that lay hidden beneath the surface of the trial.

In the end, Erin Patterson's case transcended the boundaries of a singular narrative of guilt or innocence. It became a profound exploration of the human condition, a study of the intricate interplay between motives, societal pressures, and the quiet horrors that can manifest when trust is betrayed. As the final moments of deliberation approached, the world watched, waiting for the echoes of judgment to resonate far beyond the courtroom walls.

Chapter 39: The Aftermath of Judgment — The Psychological Landscape and Social Dynamics

"The influence of social media on our perceptions of justice is a reflection of society's need for connection, validation, and sometimes, vindication." — Dr. Avery Katlin, Social Psychology Expert

I. The Weight of Financial Strain

As the jury retreated to deliberate, the psychological ramifications of financial strain loomed large over the courtroom. The relentless pressure of economic hardship can manifest in insidious ways, leading individuals to make choices that defy logic and morality. Erin Patterson's alleged actions became a case study in the psychological effects of prolonged financial strain, echoing the findings of forensic psychologists like Dr. Patrick Newton, who emphasized the interplay between financial distress and criminal behavior.

1. The Invisible Burden

Financial strain often operates beneath the surface, cloaked in shame and secrecy. Erin's mounting debts and increasingly strained relationships may have created a psychological environment where desperation flourished. This invisible burden can warp perceptions, leading individuals to rationalize extreme measures as necessary for survival. The psychological toll of such stress can lead to cognitive dissonance, where the individual struggles to reconcile their actions with their self-image. Erin might have believed that her drastic choices were justified, a misguided attempt to regain control over her chaotic life.

2. Historical Context — A Pattern of Desperation

The parallels between Erin's situation and historical cases of financial desperation leading to murder are striking. From the notorious case of John List, who killed his family to escape financial ruin, to the more recent case of the McStay family, where financial turmoil precipitated tragedy, these narratives illustrate a chilling pattern. Criminologists like Dr. Laura Pettler often emphasize that financial strain can act as a catalyst for crime, pushing otherwise ordinary individuals into the depths of moral depravity.

II. The Role of Social Media — A Double-Edged Sword

In the age of digital connectivity, social media has become a powerful force in shaping public perception and influencing individual behavior. As the world watched the Erin Patterson case unfold, platforms like Facebook and Twitter served as both a lifeline and a weapon.

1. The Faceless Supporters

Erin's online presence allowed her to cultivate a network of faceless supporters, individuals who rallied behind her without fully understanding the complexities of her situation. This virtual camaraderie can create an echo chamber, where individuals reinforce each other's beliefs and emotions. Erin's interactions with these online friends may have provided her with a distorted sense of validation, leading her to believe she had a right to her actions. The psychological phenomenon of social validation can embolden individuals, blurring the lines between right and wrong.

2. The Impact of Online Narratives

The trial generated a whirlwind of social media commentary, with hashtags like #JusticeForErin and #InnocentUntilProven trending alongside their oppositional counterparts. This digital discourse often devolved into a battleground of opinions, where nuanced discussions gave way to polarized viewpoints. Criminologists have observed that social media can amplify biases, creating a narrative that may not align with the truth. The online frenzy surrounding Erin's case may have shaped public perception, influencing not only the jury pool but also Erin's own psychological state as she navigated the terrain of public scrutiny.

3. The Case of Amanda Knox — A Comparative Analysis

Erin Patterson's experience can be likened to that of Amanda Knox, whose murder trial became a media spectacle fueled by social media narratives. Both women faced a relentless onslaught of public opinion, where their lives were dissected and judged by faceless commentators. The psychological effects of such scrutiny can be profound, leading individuals to internalize public perceptions and grapple with their identities. Knox's eventual exoneration serves as a reminder of the dangers inherent in a trial by media, echoing the warnings of forensic psychologists who caution against conflating public opinion with legal truth.

III. The Broader Implications — Crime, Judgment, and Society

As the jury prepared to deliberate, the implications of Erin Patterson's case extended beyond the courtroom, inviting society to confront its own values and beliefs about justice, morality, and the complexities of human behavior.

1. The Nature of Trust and Betrayal

Erin's alleged betrayal of familial trust raises profound questions about the nature of human relationships. The case serves as a microcosm of broader societal issues, where trust can be weaponized, and betrayal can lead to unimaginable consequences. Forensic psychologists like Dr. Tiffany Lewis emphasize the importance of understanding the psychological dynamics at play in familial relationships, particularly in cases involving domestic violence and manipulation. Erin's actions, whether premeditated or impulsive, highlight the fragility of trust within families and the potential for betrayal to spiral into tragedy.

2. Legal and Ethical Considerations

The case has ignited discussions about the legal system's ability to navigate the complexities of psychological motivations behind crimes. As the jury deliberated, questions loomed about the adequacy of the legal framework in addressing the nuances of intent, particularly in cases involving emotional and psychological manipulation. Experts like Dr. Catherine Andrews note that the legal system must evolve to reflect the realities of modern crime, recognizing the psychological dimensions that often underlie criminal behavior.

IV. The Jury's Deliberation — A Moment of Truth

As the jury began their deliberations, the courtroom held its collective breath. The verdict would serve as a reflection of not just Erin Patterson's fate but also society's understanding of trust, betrayal, and the psychological underpinnings of crime. Would the jury see her as a desperate woman driven to the brink, or as a calculating poisoner who wielded trust as a weapon?

In this charged atmosphere, the broader implications of the trial hung heavily in the air. Erin Patterson's case was not merely a legal proceeding; it was a profound exploration of the human condition, a reminder of the fragility of trust, the impact of societal pressures, and the complexities of morality in a world where the lines between right and wrong are often blurred.

As the final moments of deliberation approached, the nation awaited the verdict, poised to confront the uncomfortable truths that lay beneath the surface of the trial. Whether Erin Patterson was deemed guilty or innocent, the echoes of this case would resonate far beyond the courtroom, prompting conversations about justice, trust, and the quiet horrors that often unfold behind closed doors.

Chapter 40: A Crucible of Decision — The Jury's Journey

"The law is reason, free from passion." — Aristotle

I. The Deliberation Begins

As the heavy doors of the courtroom swung closed behind the twelve jurors, a palpable tension filled the air. The trial of Erin Patterson had reached a critical juncture, and the weight of the evidence, the emotional testimonies, and the intricate nuances of the arguments presented over the past ten weeks loomed large in the minds of those tasked with determining her fate. They were not just deciding the guilt or innocence of a woman accused of a heinous crime; they were engaging in a profound exploration of morality, trust, and the human condition.

Justice Christopher Beale's final instructions echoed in their ears. The jurors were reminded of their duty to reach a unanimous verdict—a challenging task given the complex emotional and legal landscapes they had traversed. The judge's words served as a beacon, guiding them through the tumult of evidence and emotion, encouraging them to remain focused on the facts presented before them.

II. The Jurors' Reflections — A Weighty Responsibility

The jurors, a diverse group comprising both men and women, brought their own life experiences, biases, and perspectives into the deliberation room. As they took their seats, each juror was acutely aware of the gravity of their responsibility. They had witnessed the emotional testimony of Erin Patterson, heard the harrowing accounts of the surviving family member, Ian Wilkinson, and absorbed extensive expert opinions from forensic psychologists and legal scholars.

In the privacy of their deliberation room, discussions began to unfold. Each juror shared their impressions of the evidence, dissecting the prosecution's claims that Erin had deliberately poisoned her in-laws with death cap mushrooms. The emotional weight of the trial pressed upon them as they considered the implications of their decision—not just for Erin, but for the families affected by the tragedy.

1. The Burden of Evidence

The jurors revisited the key pieces of evidence presented during the trial, including Erin's alleged lies about her health and her actions leading up to the fatal lunch. They grappled with the prosecution's assertion that Erin had intentionally sought to control the meal's ingredients, thereby enabling her to include the toxic mushrooms without detection. The intricate details of the case, including the testimonies regarding the individual plates served and Erin's behavior during the meal, were scrutinized in an attempt to discern intent.

2. The Challenge of Motive

One of the central questions facing the jurors was whether Erin had a motive strong enough to drive her to commit such a crime. The prosecution argued that financial strain and familial discord had created an environment ripe for malevolence, while the defense suggested that the absence of motive indicated a tragic accident rather than premeditated murder. Jurors debated the nuances of

Erin's character, exploring whether her claims of love for her in-laws could coexist with the possibility of murder.

III. The Influence of Social Media — A Modern Trial by Public Opinion

As the jurors deliberated, the impact of social media loomed large over their discussions. The case had attracted immense public attention, with media coverage and online commentary shaping the narrative surrounding the trial. Jurors were instructed to avoid external influences, yet the reality of living in a digitally connected world made it nearly impossible to remain untouched by the fervor surrounding Erin's case.

1. The Role of Digital Echo Chambers

With hashtags like #JusticeForErin and #InnocentUntilProven trending on social media, the lines between fact and opinion blurred. These digital echo chambers created an environment where public sentiment could sway perceptions of guilt and innocence. Jurors discussed the potential implications of this online fervor, recognizing how it could color their understanding of the case, even as they endeavored to adhere strictly to the evidence presented in court.

2. The Faceless Supporters

Erin's online support network, composed of faceless figures rallying behind her, provided her with a sense of validation. The jurors considered whether this support might have influenced Erin's own beliefs about her innocence, leading her to feel justified in her actions. In the eyes of some jurors, this online camaraderie could have fostered a dangerous sense of entitlement, blurring the moral boundaries between right and wrong.

IV. The Complexity of Deliberation — Navigating Uncertainty

As the hours passed, the jurors faced the reality of their task: reaching a unanimous verdict. Each juror brought their unique perspectives, and the discussions oscillated between certainty and doubt. The deliberation room became a microcosm of the broader societal debate surrounding trust, betrayal, and the nature of evil.

1. The Psychological Toll of Decision-Making

The psychological burden of reaching a consensus weighed heavily on the jurors. They were tasked not only with evaluating evidence but also with reconciling their own emotions regarding the case. The discussions became a reflection of the broader societal struggle with understanding the complexities of human behavior and the motivations behind seemingly incomprehensible actions.

2. The Uncertainty of Verdicts

The jurors were acutely aware that they held the power to alter the course of Erin Patterson's life. The prospect of declaring a woman guilty of murder was daunting, and many jurors grappled with the implications of their decision. The concept of "innocent until proven guilty" was a guiding principle, yet the reality of the evidence presented challenged their comfort with that notion.

V. An Unfolding Narrative — The Intersection of Law and Emotion

In the backdrop of their deliberations, the jurors began to reflect on the broader implications of the trial itself. The Erin Patterson case served as a lens through which societal attitudes toward trust, familial relationships, and the nature of evil were scrutinized. The discussions in the jury room transcended mere legal considerations; they delved into the emotional and psychological landscapes that underpin human behavior.

1. A Reflection of Society

The trial had become a mirror reflecting the complexities of modern life, where the hidden dangers of familial relationships can culminate in tragedy. The jurors considered how their verdict would resonate beyond the courtroom, shaping public discourse on domestic violence, psychological manipulation, and the consequences of betrayal.

2. The Journey Toward a Verdict

As the deliberation continued, the jurors navigated their way through the intricate web of evidence, emotion, and societal expectation. Each hour brought them closer to a decision that would echo through the lives of Erin Patterson, her family, and the community at large. The journey toward a verdict was fraught with uncertainty, yet it was also a testament to the complexities of justice in a world where morality, intent, and human emotion intertwine.

VI. Awaiting the Verdict — A Nation Holds Its Breath

As the day drew to a close, the jurors remained in their deliberation room, sequestered from the world outside. The weight of responsibility hung heavy in the air, a reminder that their decision would not only determine Erin Patterson's fate but also contribute to the ongoing dialogue about trust, betrayal, and the dark corners of human nature.

The nation watched, waited, and wondered what the jury would ultimately decide. Would they find Erin guilty of murder, or would they see her as a tragic figure caught in the web of circumstance? The answers remained elusive, shrouded in the complexities of human behavior and the intricate dance of justice, as the jury faced the daunting task of navigating the tumultuous waters of judgment.

Chapter 41: The Deliberative Silence — Between the Lines of Justice

"Justice delayed is justice denied." — William E. Gladstone

I. The Weight of Decision — A Jury in Contemplation

In the quiet confines of the jury room, the atmosphere was thick with contemplation. The twelve jurors, now fully aware of the monumental task ahead, settled into a rhythm of discussion, each grappling with the weight of their responsibility. The echoes of Justice Beale's final instructions reverberated in their minds, reminding them that the verdict must be unanimous—a daunting requirement that added to the gravity of their deliberations.

As they gathered around the table, a palpable tension hung in the air, mingling with the anticipation of what lay ahead. The jurors were acutely aware that their decision would not only impact Erin Patterson's life but also reverberate through the lives of the victims' families and the broader community. Every aspect of the case, from the emotional testimonies to the meticulous details of the evidence, was laid bare before them, demanding their utmost attention.

II. The Echo of the Judge's Words

Justice Beale had outlined the key elements the jurors needed to consider in their deliberations: Did Erin Patterson cause the deaths of her in-laws? Was there intent behind her actions? Did she act without lawful justification? These questions loomed large as they sifted through the evidence presented over the past weeks, weighing the prosecution's assertions against the defense's arguments.

1. The Complexity of Intent

The crux of the jury's deliberation rested on determining Erin's intent. They revisited the prosecution's claim that her choice to serve individual beef Wellingtons allowed her to control the ingredients, including the lethal death cap mushrooms. The jurors debated whether this constituted premeditated murder or if the incident could be explained as a tragic accident, as the defense argued.

2. The Allegations of Deceit

Justice Beale had warned them about the implications of Erin's alleged lies during her testimony. The jurors discussed the significance of these claimed fabrications, pondering whether they were indicative of guilt or simply a reflection of a woman caught in a web of circumstance. The emotional turmoil of her situation was palpable, challenging them to consider how fear and desperation might cloud judgment.

III. The Influence of Public Opinion — A Jury Under Scrutiny

Outside the jury room, the world continued to buzz with speculation and analysis. Media outlets, social platforms, and even casual conversations in cafes across Australia were dominated by the case. The trial had become a focal point of national interest, with the public eagerly awaiting the jury's verdict. The jurors were aware of the intense scrutiny they faced, not only from the media but also from the community, which had become invested in the outcome of the trial.

1. Navigating Social Pressures

The jurors were reminded of Justice Beale's explicit instructions to avoid external influences, yet they were human, and the weight of public opinion inevitably seeped into their consciousness. They discussed how the pervasive media coverage could affect their deliberation process. Would they be swayed by the narratives spun online, or could they remain steadfast in their commitment to the evidence presented in court?

2. The Responsibility of Secrecy

The jurors understood the importance of confidentiality in their deliberations, aware that the details of their discussions would never be revealed. This secrecy added an additional layer of pressure; they were tasked with reaching a consensus without revealing the nuances of their reasoning. They recognized that a hung jury could lead to a retrial, prolonging the anguish for all involved.

IV. The Emotional Landscape — Grappling with Morality

As discussions progressed, the jurors delved deeper into the emotional landscape of the case. The profound themes of trust, betrayal, and the complexities of familial relationships echoed throughout their deliberations. They reflected on Erin's role as a mother and daughter-in-law, attempting to reconcile her character with the possibility of murder.

1. **The Bonds of Family**

Some jurors expressed sympathy for Erin, considering her claims of love for her in-laws and the emotional toll of the situation. They debated whether it was plausible that a loving mother could commit such a heinous act. The intricacies of familial bonds and the potential for betrayal added layers of complexity to their discussions, challenging them to confront their own beliefs about morality and justice.

2. **The Nature of Evil**

The jurors grappled with the broader philosophical implications of the case. What does it mean to be a murderer? Can one be driven to kill through desperation and fear rather than a fundamental evil? These questions became central to their deliberations, forcing them to confront uncomfortable truths about human nature and the capacity for darkness that exists within us all.

V. Anticipation of a Verdict — The Road Ahead

As the day wore on, the jurors continued to engage in spirited discussions, each contributing their thoughts and perspectives. The deliberation process was not without its challenges; moments of disagreement arose, yet they were met with a mutual respect that underscored the gravity of their task.

1. **The Uncertainty of Time**

With deliberations set to continue daily from Monday to Saturday, the jurors understood that time was both an ally and an adversary. Each moment spent in discussion brought them closer to a resolution, yet the uncertainty of the timeline weighed heavily on their minds. They were aware that the decision they reached would have lasting implications for Erin Patterson, the victims' families, and the broader community.

2. A Nation Awaits

Outside the jury room, the nation held its breath, waiting for the verdict that would determine Erin Patterson's fate. Media outlets buzzed with speculation, while social media trends reflected the divided opinions surrounding the case. Would the jury find her guilty of murder, or would they see her as a tragic figure caught in a web of circumstance? The answers remained elusive, shrouded in the complexities of human behavior and the intricate dance of justice.

As the jurors prepared to continue their discussions, the weight of their decision loomed large. They were not just judging a woman accused of a crime; they were wading into the depths of morality, trust, and the profound consequences of human actions. The deliberation room had become a sanctuary for exploration, a space where the fundamental questions of justice and humanity collided, and the outcome remained a tantalizing mystery.

Chapter 42: The Verdict — A Reflection on Guilt and the Nature of Evil

"Evil is not a force; it is a choice." — Dr. Helen Morrison

I. The Calm Before the Storm

As the jury continued its deliberations on this fateful day, July 1st, 2025, the atmosphere in the courtroom was thick with anticipation. Outside, the world was abuzz with speculation as media outlets and social media platforms dissected every detail of the ongoing trial. But within the jury room, a profound silence reigned—a silence that belied the intense discussions taking place just beyond the walls.

In the wake of the evidence presented over the past weeks, I could not shake the feeling that the scales of justice were tipping toward a guilty verdict for Erin Patterson. My years of experience studying human behavior, particularly within the realm of low-visibility offenses, guided my understanding of the intricacies surrounding this case. The patterns of deception, the psychological markers of intent, and the chilling reality of poison as a method of murder all coalesced into a narrative that, in my estimation, pointed firmly towards guilt.

II. A Case Built on Shadows — The Evidence of Guilt

From the moment the trial began, it became clear that Erin Patterson's life was a tapestry woven with complexity and contradiction. The prosecution's case relied on a series of compelling threads, each one highlighting her alleged premeditated actions on that fatal day in July 2023.

1. The Premeditation Theory

The prosecution argued that Erin deliberately selected death cap mushrooms, a toxic fungus known for its lethal potential, and incorporated them into the beef Wellington served to her in-laws. This theory aligned with Dr. Katherine Ramsland's script theory, which posits that offenders often rehearse their actions like actors preparing for a role. Every detail—from the choice of meal to the alleged lies about her health—seemed to fit a carefully constructed narrative, one designed to mask her true intentions.

2. Consciousness of Guilt

John Douglas's principles of behavioral profiling illuminated the digital breadcrumbs left in the wake of Erin's actions. The deleted search histories and inconsistent statements served as markers of a consciousness of guilt. These were not mere oversights; they were calculated moves meant to obscure the truth. The evidence presented in court clearly indicated that Erin had something to hide, and the jury must have grappled with the implications of this evidence as they deliberated.

3. The Complexity of Poisoning

Poisoners, as noted by Dr. Helen Morrison, often embody a chilling duality. They appear to be caregivers, yet they wield the power to end lives with a seemingly benign act. Erin's alleged actions reflected this complexity, as she navigated the delicate balance between love and malice. The notion that someone could poison their own family while maintaining an appearance of normalcy is one of the most unsettling aspects of this case and one that undoubtedly weighed heavily on the jury's minds.

III. The Psychological Landscape — Understanding Erin's Mindset

As I dissected the case, I could not help but reflect on the psychological pressures that may have influenced Erin's alleged actions. The pressures of financial instability, the isolation from her in-laws, and the unraveling of her marriage created a perfect storm for desperation.

1. The Erosion of Identity

Erin's identity as a mother, wife, and daughter-in-law had been undermined by her circumstances. Dr. Laura Nicholls' research into narcissistic rage and identity fragmentation spoke to the potential for a slow, internal corrosion that could lead an individual to commit unspeakable acts. Erin's alleged choice to poison those closest to her was not just an act of violence; it was a manifestation of her struggle to reclaim control over a life that felt increasingly chaotic.

2. The Theoretical Framework

Throughout my career, I have immersed myself in the teachings of the world's foremost minds in criminal psychology. The works of Clarissa Jenevra and Dr. Rachel Monroe provided valuable insights into the nature of poisoners as "masters of dual reality." They highlight how these individuals can simultaneously embody empathy while exhibiting cold calculation. Erin's case, if proven guilty, would exemplify this disturbing paradox, showcasing the complexities of human nature.

IV. The Public's Eye — The Role of Media and Social Commentary

The trial of Erin Patterson had captivated the nation, drawing in media coverage that transformed the courtroom into a public spectacle. The relentless scrutiny from the press and the public discourse surrounding the case added layers of complexity to the jury's deliberation process.

1. The Influence of Social Media

As the jury weighed their decision, they were undoubtedly aware of the public sentiment swirling around Erin's case. The digital age has intensified the pressures faced by jurors, as social media platforms amplify opinions and narratives that may not align with the facts presented in court. The potential for bias, fueled by the noise of public opinion, posed a significant challenge to their task of remaining impartial.

2. The Dichotomy of Public Sentiment

The juxtaposition of support for Erin alongside calls for justice for the victims reflected the broader societal struggle with understanding trust and betrayal in familial relationships. Would the jury be swayed by the emotional resonance of public opinion, or would they remain steadfast in their commitment to the evidence? The answer to this question held profound implications for the trial's outcome.

V. The Impending Verdict — A Reflection on Justice and Morality

As I contemplated the possible verdict, I found myself grappling with the broader implications of the case. The Erin Patterson trial was not merely a legal proceeding; it was a cultural touchstone that illuminated the complexities of human behavior and the nature of evil.

1.   A Reflection of Societal Values

The verdict would serve as a reflection of societal values, forcing us to confront the uncomfortable truths about trust, manipulation, and the potential for violence that lurks beneath the surface of domestic life. As the jury prepared to reach a decision, the nation held its breath, awaiting a verdict that would resonate far beyond the courtroom.

2.   The Responsibility of Judgment

The jury's decision would carry with it the weight of responsibility—not just for Erin Patterson, but for the families affected, the community of Leongatha, and the broader societal discourse on domestic violence and trust. As they entered the final stages of deliberation, I could not help but feel that their verdict would serve as a pivotal moment in understanding how we navigate the complexities of human relationships and the choices that can lead to tragedy.

VI. Conclusion — The Shadow of Doubt

As the sun set on July 1st, 2025, the jury continued its deliberations, and I found myself reflecting on the myriad of factors that shaped this case. While I believed Erin Patterson would ultimately be found guilty, the uncertainties surrounding intent, the interplay of emotions, and the societal implications made this trial a profound exploration of the human psyche.

In the end, the Erin Patterson case serves as a cautionary tale, a reminder that beneath the surface of mundane domesticity lies a potential for darkness that can manifest in the most unexpected ways. Whether the jury finds Erin guilty or not, this case will leave an indelible mark on our understanding of crime, trust, and the human condition. The truth, however elusive, beckons us to consider the patterns that lie hidden beneath the surface and the chilling reality that anyone—given the right set of circumstances— might be capable of crossing the line.

Chapter 43: The Verdict — Unraveling the Mind of a Murderer

"Evil is not a force; it is a choice, an action taken in cold calculation." — Rusty Le Grande

I. The Day of Reckoning

On July 7, 2025, the courtroom held its breath as the jury announced their verdict: Erin Patterson was found guilty of murdering her in-laws, Don and Gail Patterson, and Gail's sister, Heather Wilkinson. She was also convicted of the attempted murder of Ian Wilkinson, the sole survivor of the lunch that turned deadly. The trial had captivated Australia, and as the verdict echoed through the halls of the Morwell courthouse, the weight of this moment settled over the nation.

The proceedings had been a lengthy and complex journey, marked by emotional testimonies, forensic analysis, and a wealth of evidence that painted a damning portrait of Erin. The prosecution had meticulously presented their case, arguing that Erin had knowingly purchased and prepared death cap mushrooms, serving them to her unsuspecting guests with malicious intent.

II. The Evidence of Premeditation

The conviction was not merely the consequence of circumstantial evidence; it was the result of a comprehensive examination of Erin Patterson's actions leading up to the fateful lunch.

1. **The Forensic Trail**

The jury was presented with critical evidence, including Erin's online purchases of death cap mushrooms, her history of foraging, and the meticulous preparation of the beef Wellington. The prosecution argued that these actions demonstrated intent, a claim bolstered by forensic analysis that confirmed the presence of the toxic fungi in the meal. Erin's inconsistent statements about her mushroom foraging and her lies regarding her health only added to the narrative of guilt.

2. Behavioral Inconsistencies

The prosecution highlighted Erin's behavioral inconsistencies as significant markers of guilt. Her emotional testimony during the trial was juxtaposed with CCTV footage showing her in the days following the lunch, purchasing a sandwich while claiming to suffer from mushroom poisoning symptoms. This dissonance resonated with the principles articulated by John Douglas, emphasizing the importance of behavioral consistency in assessing intent.

3. Critical Errors

Erin Patterson's critical errors ultimately led to her downfall. Her decision to purchase the mushrooms online, coupled with her failure to adequately dispose of incriminating evidence, raised suspicions and led investigators directly to her doorstep. The prosecution argued that her lies to family and friends about the meal and ingredients further eroded her credibility, presenting a clear picture of a woman who underestimated the severity of her actions and the efficacy of the investigation.

III. The Psychological Landscape of a Killer

As I reflected on the verdict, the psychological themes that emerged throughout the trial painted a complex picture of Erin Patterson—a woman whose actions appeared to stem from a confluence of desperation, manipulation, and premeditated malice.

1. The Burden of Expectations

Erin's life had been marred by low self-esteem, financial struggles, and familial discord. Dr. Laura Nicholls' insights into identity fragmentation illuminated how these pressures could lead someone to view their loved ones as obstacles rather than family. Erin's alleged choice to poison her in-laws could be seen as a desperate attempt to reclaim control over a life spiraling out of her grasp.

2. The Duality of Evil

The case exemplified the duality of evil as noted by Dr. Helen Morrison. Erin Patterson, a mother and caregiver, was accused of committing an act so heinous that it shattered the very fabric of familial trust. The idea that someone could poison their own family while maintaining an appearance of normalcy struck at the heart of our understanding of morality.

3. The Role of Manipulation

Dr. Katherine Ramsland's script theory provided insight into Erin's behavior. Her crafting of a narrative around her illness and her actions suggested a calculated effort to manipulate those around her, portraying herself as a victim rather than a perpetrator. This manipulation of narrative is often a hallmark of individuals who commit low-visibility offenses, using deception as a shield against accountability.

IV. The Public Fascination — A Reflection of Society

The trial's outcome reverberated beyond the courtroom, prompting discussions about the nature of evil and the complexities of human relationships.

1. A Civics Lesson in Justice

The Erin Patterson trial served as a civics lesson, illustrating the intricacies of the legal system and the importance of due process. Observing the jury's deliberation highlighted the weight of responsibility jurors bear when determining guilt or innocence, reinforcing the notion that justice is a living, breathing entity that requires vigilance.

2. The Broader Implications

The public's interest in the case demonstrated a collective yearning for clarity in a world often clouded by misinformation and uncertainty. As Malcolm Knox noted, the trial became a trivia of sorts, reflecting our desire to discern fact from falsehood. The fixation on Erin Patterson's case highlighted the complexities of trust and betrayal within familial relationships and the dangers that can arise from desperation.

V. The Road Ahead — What Lies Beyond the Verdict

With the jury's decision rendered, Erin Patterson faced a new chapter—potential life in prison. The implications of the verdict would resonate far beyond the courtroom, impacting families and communities alike.

1. The Impact on Families

The Patterson and Wilkinson families had endured immense suffering, and the verdict brought a measure of closure while also raising questions about healing and reconciliation. The community of Leongatha grappled with the aftermath of the trial, reflecting on the fragility of trust within familial bonds.

2. The Evolution of Justice

Erin Patterson's case would undoubtedly inform future discussions about domestic violence, psychological manipulation, and the complexities of crime. As legal experts and criminologists continued to analyze the trial's implications, it became clear that the case would serve as a vital reference point for understanding the nuances of human behavior and the nature of evil.

VI. Conclusion — A Legacy of Lessons Learned

As the dust settled on the verdict, the Erin Patterson trial left an indelible mark on our understanding of crime, trust, and the human condition. It served as a powerful reminder that the most dangerous offenders are not always those who strike in rage but those who plan, plot, and poison with quiet intent.

In the end, the trial was not just about Erin Patterson's actions; it was a reflection of our society's values, a testament to the complexities of human relationships, and a poignant exploration of the shadows that can exist within even the most familiar of settings. As we move forward, we must remain vigilant, recognizing that the capacity for darkness exists within us all, waiting for the right circumstances to emerge. The story of Erin Patterson challenges us to confront our assumptions, question our biases, and strive for a deeper understanding of the human experience.

Chapter 44: The Aftermath — Reflections on a Community in Crisis

"Justice served is not just about punishment; it is about healing for those left behind." — Rusty Le Grande

I. The Community in Mourning

In the wake of Erin Patterson's conviction, the communities of Korumburra and Leongatha were left grappling with the aftermath. The trial had exposed the intricate dynamics of familial relationships, and the verdict sent shockwaves through a community that had been deeply affected by the tragedy. Residents struggled to reconcile the image of a mother and caregiver with the reality of a woman convicted of orchestrating a horrific act of violence against her own family.

1. The Impact on Local Families

The Patterson and Wilkinson families had suffered immeasurable loss. The deaths of Don, Gail, and Heather weighed heavily on the hearts of those who knew them. Friends and neighbors expressed their condolences, mourning not only the victims but also the shattered trust that had once defined their relationships. The community's grief was palpable, a collective sorrow that underscored the impact of the trial on their daily lives.

2. Calls for Community Awareness

The trial raised important questions about the nature of community and the importance of vigilance in relationships. Residents expressed concerns about the potential for similar crimes in the future, highlighting the need for increased awareness and support systems. The tragedy served as a stark reminder that darkness can lurk beneath the surface of even the most ordinary lives, prompting calls for open dialogue and community engagement.

II. The Personal Toll on Simon Patterson and His Children

Simon Patterson found himself in an impossible position: the estranged husband of Erin and the son of the victims. His journey through the trial was marked by profound emotional turmoil, and the verdict brought both relief and anguish.

1. Navigating Grief and Trauma

Simon openly discussed the emotional pain and trauma he had experienced throughout the trial. The loss of his parents and the betrayal of his wife had left him reeling. In the wake of the verdict, he contemplated sharing his story in a public forum, perhaps through a podcast or a book, to provide support to others affected by similar tragedies. His desire to find a voice in the aftermath of such profound loss spoke to the resilience of the human spirit.

2. The Impact on Erin's Children

The children of Erin Patterson faced their own challenges in the wake of the verdict. The fallout from their mother's actions would shape their lives in ways they could not yet comprehend. As they navigated the complexities of family dynamics and societal perceptions, the need for support and understanding became increasingly apparent.

III. Life in Prison — A New Reality for Erin Patterson

With the verdict rendered, Erin Patterson faced the grim reality of a life sentence. The implications of her actions would now manifest in the harsh environment of prison life.

1. Navigating the Prison System

Erin's status as a convicted murderer would subject her to skepticism and hostility from fellow inmates. The prison environment would likely be challenging, necessitating adaptation to strict rules and regulations. Reports indicated that she might be housed in isolation for her own protection, a situation that would limit her access to privileges and exacerbate the emotional toll of incarceration.

2. The Psychological Challenges of Incarceration

As Erin adjusted to her new reality, the psychological challenges of prison life would weigh heavily on her. The isolation and scrutiny from prison authorities would demand resilience and coping strategies. The environment, governed by strict regulations, would serve as a stark reminder of the consequences of her actions.

IV. The Broader Implications — Lessons Learned

The case of Erin Patterson serves as a multifaceted exploration of crime, trust, and the human condition. The trial has illuminated the complexities of human behavior and the factors that can lead individuals to commit unspeakable acts.

1. Understanding the Nature of Evil

Erin Patterson's actions compel us to confront the uncomfortable truths about the capacity for evil that exists within us all. The psychological theories surrounding her behavior, from the duality of poisoners to the manipulation of narrative, challenge us to reconsider our assumptions about morality and intent.

2. **The Ongoing Dialogue on Domestic Violence**

The verdict has prompted essential discussions about domestic violence and the complexities of familial relationships. As society grapples with these issues, the Erin Patterson case serves as a reminder of the importance of vigilance, understanding, and support in navigating the intricacies of human interaction.

V. Conclusion — A Community in Transition

As the dust settled on the trial, the communities of Korumburra and Leongatha faced the reality of a new chapter. The Erin Patterson case would leave an indelible mark on their collective consciousness, shaping their understanding of trust, betrayal, and the potential for darkness that exists within even the most familiar of settings.

In the end, the story of Erin Patterson is not merely a cautionary tale but a profound exploration of the complexities of human nature. It challenges us to confront our biases, question our assumptions, and strive for a deeper understanding of the human experience. As we move forward, we must remain vigilant, recognizing the capacity for darkness that can emerge in the shadows of our lives—a reminder that the most dangerous offenders are often those who operate within the confines of familiarity.

Chapter 45: The Awaited Sentencing — A Community in Reflection

"Justice is a delicate balance; it requires both accountability and understanding." — Rusty Le Grande

I. The Calm Before the Storm

As the dust settled on the verdict, the focus shifted to the impending sentencing of Erin Patterson. Found guilty of triple murder and attempted murder, Erin now awaited the judge's decision, a moment that would bring closure to a trial that had captivated the nation. The courtroom, once filled with the tension of deliberation, now buzzed with discussions of what the future might hold for Erin and the community she had left in turmoil.

While the exact date of the sentencing hearing remained uncertain, the atmosphere was thick with anticipation. Residents of Korumburra and Leongatha, deeply affected by the tragedy, found themselves grappling with a myriad of emotions—grief, anger, and a desire for justice. The trial had unveiled the complexities of familial relationships, and the community was left to ponder the impact of Erin's actions on their lives.

II. The Community's Response

As Erin awaited her fate, the local community engaged in conversations about justice, mental health, and the fragility of trust within families. The trial had forced them to confront uncomfortable truths about the nature of evil that can hide behind familiar facades.

1. **Public Sentiment**

Many community members expressed their opinions on social media and local forums, sharing their thoughts on what an appropriate sentence would be for Erin. The general sentiment leaned toward a desire for accountability, with many calling for a life sentence without the possibility of parole. The collective grief for the victims weighed heavily on their hearts, and they sought justice not just for the deceased but for the emotional scars left behind.

2. **The Role of Awareness**

The case had sparked discussions about mental health and the pressures that can lead individuals to commit acts of violence. Community leaders began organizing forums to raise awareness about domestic violence, mental health resources, and the importance of supporting one another. The tragedy had opened doors for dialogue, urging residents to engage with the complexities of human behavior and the factors that contribute to violent actions.

III. *The Psychological Implications of the Case*

As Erin Patterson's story continued to unfold, the psychological aspects of her actions became increasingly relevant. Experts weighed in on the implications of her behavior, offering insights into the mind of a convicted murderer.

1. **Understanding the Mind of a Killer**

The case drew attention from criminologists and psychologists, who analyzed Erin's motivations and mental state. Theories surrounding her actions pointed to a combination of psychological distress, desperation, and premeditated malice. Dr. Laura Nicholls and Dr. Helen Morrison's research on the psychological profiles of poisoners provided a framework for understanding the duality of Erin's character—a mother who could simultaneously embody love and malice.

2. The Complexity of Domestic Relationships

Erin's case highlighted the intricate dynamics of domestic relationships, raising questions about the pressures that can lead individuals to commit unthinkable acts. The trial had exposed the hidden struggles within families, prompting discussions about the importance of seeking help and understanding the signs of emotional distress.

IV. The Sentencing Hearing on the Horizon

While the exact date for the sentencing hearing was not yet determined, both the prosecution and defense prepared for the upcoming court session. The prosecution was expected to advocate for a severe sentence, emphasizing the premeditated nature of Erin's actions and the irreparable harm caused to the victims and their families.

1. Arguments Anticipated

The defense, on the other hand, was likely to argue for leniency, citing Erin's mental health struggles and the harsh realities of prison life. They would attempt to paint a picture of a woman overwhelmed by her circumstances, seeking to elicit sympathy from the judge. The upcoming hearing promised to be another emotionally charged moment in a saga that had already unfolded with dramatic flair.

2. **Community Vigilance**

As the hearing approached, the community remained vigilant, eager for justice to be served. Discussions about the potential outcomes of the sentencing filled the air, and residents expressed their hopes for a decision that would honor the memory of the victims. The need for closure was palpable, and the community rallied in support of the families affected by the tragedy.

V. Conclusion — A Moment of Reckoning

As Erin Patterson awaited her sentencing, the narrative surrounding her actions continued to unfold. This was a moment of reflection for the community, a time to grapple with the complexities of human behavior and the fragility of trust.

The impact of the trial would resonate far beyond the courtroom, serving as a reminder of the challenges that families face and the need for greater awareness and support. As the community prepared for the next chapter in this harrowing tale, they understood that justice must not only be served but also understood in the context of the human experience.

Chapter 46: The Path Forward — Navigating the Aftermath of Tragedy

"Even in the darkest moments, there is a light to be found in healing and understanding." — Rusty Le Grande

I. Preparing for the Sentencing Hearing

As the date for Erin Patterson's sentencing hearing drew closer, the community began to prepare for the implications of the decision. Conversations shifted from the trial itself to what the future might hold for Erin, her family, and the families of the victims. The upcoming hearing would not only determine Erin's fate but also set the tone for community healing.

1. Community Support Initiatives

In the wake of the trial, local leaders and organizations began to establish support initiatives aimed at addressing the emotional fallout from the tragedy. Counseling sessions and community forums were organized, allowing residents to discuss their feelings, share their stories, and support one another in the healing process. This collective effort served as a reminder that even in the face of darkness, the community could come together to seek understanding and solace.

2. The Role of Education

The trial had opened the door to a broader conversation about the need for education surrounding domestic violence, mental health, and the signs of distress. Schools and community centers began implementing programs aimed at raising awareness and equipping individuals with the tools to recognize and address issues before they escalate. This proactive approach highlighted the community's commitment to preventing future tragedies.

II. The Broader Implications of the Case

Erin Patterson's case had captured national attention, and as it moved toward sentencing, discussions about its implications continued to gain momentum. The case was not just about a single act of violence; it was a reflection of societal issues that resonated deeply.

1. Understanding Domestic Dynamics

The complexities of domestic relationships were brought to the forefront, prompting experts to analyze the factors that can lead to violence within families. Discussions about power dynamics, emotional manipulation, and societal pressures served as a reminder that anyone could become entangled in a web of dysfunction. The need for compassion and understanding was emphasized, urging individuals to seek help rather than resort to harmful actions.

2. The Importance of Mental Health Awareness

Erin's mental health struggles became a focal point for discussions about the need for accessible mental health resources. The case underscored the importance of addressing mental health as a critical component of overall well-being. Advocacy groups began pushing for increased funding and support for mental health initiatives, recognizing that prevention and treatment could play a vital role in reducing violence.

III. The Emotional Toll on Simon Patterson and His Children

As the community rallied for healing, Simon Patterson found himself at the center of a personal journey through grief and trauma. The estranged husband of Erin and son of the victims, Simon faced the daunting task of navigating the aftermath of the trial while supporting his children.

1. The Struggle for Understanding

Simon opened up about his emotional pain, expressing a desire to make sense of the tragedy that had upended his life. He contemplated sharing his story through various mediums—perhaps a podcast or a book—hoping to provide insight and support to others who had experienced similar loss. His determination to find meaning in the chaos served as a testament to the resilience of the human spirit.

2. Coping with Grief

The impact of Erin's actions extended to Simon's children, who faced their own challenges in the wake of the trial. The emotional toll of losing their grandparents while grappling with their mother's conviction weighed heavily on them. As a family, they sought counseling and support, recognizing the importance of addressing their grief head-on.

IV. The Sentencing Hearing on the Horizon

As the community prepared for the sentencing hearing, Erin Patterson's fate hung in the balance. The discussions surrounding the hearing became a focal point for residents, who eagerly awaited the judge's decision.

1. **Arguments Anticipated**

The prosecution was expected to emphasize the premeditated nature of Erin's actions, calling for life imprisonment without the possibility of parole. Conversely, the defense would likely argue for leniency, citing Erin's mental health struggles and the harsh realities of prison life. The courtroom would once again become a battleground, and the community watched closely.

2. **A Reflection on Justice**

The upcoming hearing served as a reminder of the complexities of justice. As the community awaited the judge's decision, they understood that this moment would not only impact Erin but also shape their understanding of accountability and healing.

V. Conclusion — A Community United in Healing

As Erin Patterson awaited her sentencing, the community of Korumburra and Leongatha stood at a crossroads. The events surrounding the trial had prompted deep reflection on trust, betrayal, and the challenges of human relationships.

The path forward was unclear, but the community was united in its commitment to healing. They understood that while justice must be served, it was equally important to foster understanding and support among one another. The tragedy had opened doors for dialogue and growth, and as they moved forward, the community would strive to emerge stronger, more aware, and resilient in the face of adversity.

In the end, Erin's story was not just a cautionary tale; it was a call to action—a reminder of the importance of compassion, awareness, and the ongoing pursuit of justice in a world that often feels chaotic and uncertain.

Chapter 47: A Personal Reflection on the Verdict

"Justice is not merely about punishing the guilty; it is a profound responsibility to society and the memory of those lost." — Rusty Le Grande

I. The Weight of the Verdict

After the jury delivered their verdict, I found myself reflecting on the implications of Erin Patterson's conviction. The trial had been a harrowing journey, one that exposed the darker sides of human nature and the complexities of familial relationships. Having watched the evidence unfold, I firmly believe that Erin Patterson is not just guilty; she is a mass murderer who deserves to serve life in prison without the possibility of parole.

1. The Evidence Against Erin

The jury deliberated for seven days, an unusually lengthy process that underscored the gravity of the case. While they had no questions during their deliberation—a testament to the clarity of the prosecution's argument—the evidence presented was damning: Erin had purchased death cap mushrooms online, prepared them, and served them in a meal that ultimately killed three people and nearly claimed a fourth life. Her lies to friends and family about the meal, coupled with her inconsistent statements, painted a clear picture of someone who had knowingly engaged in a premeditated act of violence.

2. The Nature of the Crime

Although the prosecution could not definitively prove a motive, the jury's verdict emphasized the impact of Erin's actions on the victims and their families. The tragedy was not just a culinary misadventure; it was a deliberate act that shattered lives and left a community grappling with the aftermath of betrayal. The evidence made it abundantly clear: Erin Patterson had orchestrated a horrific crime, and she should be held accountable.

II. The Sentencing — Anticipation of Consequences

As the sentencing hearing approaches, I am fully aware of the arguments both sides will present. The prosecution will likely advocate for a life sentence, emphasizing the premeditated nature of Erin's actions and the irreparable harm caused to the victims' families. Conversely, the defense will probably call for leniency, citing her mental health struggles and the harsh realities of prison life.

1. Expected Arguments

I have no doubt that the defense will attempt to paint Erin as a troubled woman who succumbed to overwhelming pressures. However, this argument falls flat in light of the premeditated nature of her crime. The psychological evaluations presented during the trial should not excuse her behavior but rather highlight the need for accountability.

2. The Likelihood of an Appeal

In my estimation, the defense will pursue an appeal, as is standard in high-profile cases, but I believe such an attempt is unlikely to be successful. The evidence against Erin is too strong, and the jury's decision was reached after careful consideration of the facts. As the community awaits the judge's sentencing decision, I stand firm in my belief that justice must be served.

III. The Broader Context — Comparing Infamous Cases

As I reflect on Erin Patterson's actions, I cannot help but draw comparisons to other infamous murder cases that have captivated the public's attention. The nature of her crimes resonates with some of the most notorious cases in Australia and beyond, and I believe that Erin Patterson is every bit as culpable as the individuals involved in these high-profile tragedies.

1. The Lindy Chamberlain Case

The case of Lindy Chamberlain, whose baby Azaria was believed to have been taken by a dingo, is a poignant example of how public perception can be shaped by tragedy. Lindy was wrongfully convicted of murder, and her case highlighted the dangers of jumping to conclusions in the absence of concrete evidence. While Erin's case diverges in many ways, both trials showcase the complexities of familial relationships and the societal need for resolution in the face of tragedy.

2. The Disappearance of Peter Falconio

The case of British tourist Peter Falconio, who vanished in the Australian outback, is another chilling reminder of the violence that can lurk beneath the surface of everyday life. His suspected murder at the hands of Bradley Murdoch remains unresolved, echoing Erin Patterson's case in its impact on the national consciousness. Both cases serve as reminders of the fragility of life and the darkness that can arise in unexpected circumstances.

3. **Global Comparisons**

Moreover, Erin Patterson's case has drawn international attention, similar to other notorious poisoners and family annihilators throughout history. The calculated nature of her actions places her alongside individuals like Graham Young and Stella Nickell, both of whom engaged in heinous acts of violence cloaked in domesticity. Erin Patterson, in her own right, will forever be remembered as a killer and a mass murderer.

IV. Conclusion — The Enduring Legacy of the Case

As I pen these final chapters, I am left with a profound sense of responsibility. The Erin Patterson case transcends the courtroom; it is a reflection of society's values, a testament to the complexities of human relationships, and a stark reminder of the potential for darkness that exists within us all.

This case has sparked essential conversations about trust, mental health, and the need for community vigilance. It serves as a cautionary tale, urging us to recognize the signs of distress and to extend compassion to those who may be struggling. Yet, it also reinforces the necessity of accountability for those who commit acts of violence, ensuring that justice is served for the lives lost.

As we move forward, we must remember that the pursuit of justice is not just about retribution; it is about healing, understanding, and fostering a society that values life and compassion. The legacy of Erin Patterson's actions will linger, and it is up to us to ensure that the lessons learned from this tragedy contribute to a more just and empathetic community.

In closing, I stand resolute in my belief: Erin Patterson is guilty, and she must face the consequences of her actions. It is a truth that must be acknowledged, and as we await the final verdict on her sentencing, we must commit ourselves to understanding the depths of human behavior and the complex realities that underpin acts of violence.

Chapter 48: The Anticipation of Sentencing — A Lasting Reflection

"The truth of a crime is not just in the act itself, but in the ripples it creates through society." — Rusty Le Grande

I. The Calm Before the Sentence

As this story goes to publication, the nation holds its breath in anticipation of Erin Patterson's sentencing. Found guilty of triple murder and attempted murder, Erin's future remains uncertain, and the collective emotions of the community and the country are palpable. The trial has been a harrowing journey that exposed the darker sides of human nature and the complexities of familial relationships, leaving many to ponder the implications of her actions.

1. **The Weight of the Verdict**

Following the jury's deliberation, which lasted an unusually long seven days, the evidence presented against Erin was damning. She had purchased death cap mushrooms online, prepared them, and served them in a meal that ultimately killed three people and nearly claimed a fourth life. Her lies to friends and family about the meal, along with her inconsistent statements, painted a clear picture of someone who engaged in a premeditated act of violence.

2. **The Nature of the Crime**

While the prosecution could not definitively prove a motive, the jury's verdict emphasized the profound impact of Erin's actions on her victims and their families. This was not merely a tragic culinary misadventure; it was a calculated act that shattered lives and left a community grappling with the aftermath of betrayal. Erin Patterson's legacy is now forever intertwined with the narrative of loss and suffering she created.

II. The Waiting Game — A Nation in Reflection

As the country awaits the sentencing hearing, discussions surrounding Erin's case have intensified. The courtroom drama, which captivated audiences during the trial, has left many eager for closure, and the anticipated sentence has become a topic of national conversation.

1. Public Sentiment

The sentiment surrounding Erin's impending sentencing leans heavily toward a desire for accountability. Many believe she should face life in prison without the possibility of parole, a fitting consequence for the premeditated nature of her actions. The community has expressed a strong need for justice, not just for the lives lost but for the emotional scars left on those who loved them.

2. The Role of Awareness

This case has ignited crucial conversations about mental health, trust, and the complexities of familial relationships. Community leaders are beginning to organize forums to raise awareness about domestic violence and the importance of recognizing signs of distress in those around us. Erin's actions have opened the door for dialogue, urging individuals to engage with these difficult topics and seek help when needed.

III. The Broader Context — A Reflection on Society

As I reflect on the Erin Patterson case, it is evident that her actions resonate with notable tragedies both domestically and internationally. The public's fascination with her case mirrors the broader societal issues surrounding violence, trust, and betrayal.

1. A Reflection of Societal Values

Erin Patterson's case has prompted a national introspection about the nature of evil and the complexities of human relationships. It serves as a reminder that individuals can harbor dark intentions beneath a veneer of normalcy. The trial has exposed the uncomfortable truth that violence can emerge from within our own families, challenging us to confront our assumptions about those we hold dear.

2. Lessons from the Tragedy

The aftermath of Erin's actions will undoubtedly shape future discussions about accountability and the need for vigilance in our communities. This case has become a touchstone for understanding the psychological factors that can lead to such devastating choices. It urges us to consider the importance of support systems, mental health resources, and open conversations about the struggles people may face in silence.

IV. Conclusion — The Enduring Impact of a Tragedy

As the world awaits the outcome of Erin Patterson's sentencing, the narrative surrounding her actions continues to evolve. The events of this trial serve as a reminder of the complexities of human nature and the delicate balance between trust and betrayal.

While Erin's case is undeniably tragic, it has sparked vital discussions about mental health, societal responsibility, and the importance of community support. The legacy of her actions will linger, reminding us that within the fabric of our lives, we must be vigilant against the darkness that can emerge in familiar settings.

As we move forward, we must remain committed to fostering a society that values life, seeks understanding, and stands firm in the pursuit of justice. The Erin Patterson story is a cautionary tale, one that urges us to confront our assumptions and engage with the complexities of the human experience. Ultimately, justice must be served, and the lessons learned from this tragedy should guide us toward a more compassionate and aware community.

9 781764 108720